LET'S GO HIKING

FIRST SERIES

Twelve Walking Tour Itineraries in England and Wales

By
GORDON COOPER

PREFACE

By CLOUGH WILLIAMS-ELLIS, F.R.I.B.A., M.T.P.I.

" LET'S GO HIKING "—or, as I should have said fifty years ago when the hills first beckoned me to explore them—" What about a walk? ", though as often as not I said it to myself alone.

Maybe that is where Hiking and Rambling differ from mere walking, implying, as they seem to do, a certain measure of companionable co-operation, forethought and organisation, without which there are many who would never penetrate far into those wilds and solitudes that are reserved for the sole delight of leg-users.

Myself, for the very best country, I like solitude and silence, to be all eyes, with my ears alert only for sounds of wind and water and birds. But approaching and leaving such scenic sanctuaries, I welcome a congenial escort and the good conversation that walking does seem to promote. Yet, once arrived in Arcady, I feel like crying out, " Ladies and gentlemen, pray silence for the view ". So perhaps I am only a Relative Rambler—a mere Half-Hiker, and therefore but poorly qualified to introduce such a book as Mr. Cooper's.

Except that I love our English countryside—most dearly of all when it is Welsh.

As a member of the Government National Parks Committee, I have seen more of it in the past twelve months than—too often—in as many years. Yet I still recall delightful walks from London with " The Sunday Tramps ", ingeniously mapped out and led through the Home Counties that are now (untruly) said to have become " all home and no county ".

Where Mr. Cooper proposes to take you I have not the least idea, as I have not seen his book. But with his experience he ought to be a good guide. Try him and see.

CLOUGH WILLIAMS-ELLIS.

FOREWORD

In the preparation of this book I owe much to help and advice received from others.

First and foremost, the discussions, suggestions and assistance given me by J. H. Ingram have been invaluable. I owe him my deepest thanks. Mr. Boggis of the R.A.C. has also given me much useful advice.

Every care has been taken to check up the place-names, distances, etc. If errors have inadvertently occurred the blame is mine, and I would be most obliged if those who have comments, criticisms, and suggestions would communicate them to me.

The maps contained in this book are based upon the Ordnance Survey, with the sanction of the Controller of H.M. Stationery Office.

I hope the reader will get as much pleasure from exploring England and Wales as I have. If this book serves to whet the interest of would-be hikers, I am sure they will never regret it.

GORDON COOPER

.

CONTENTS

	PAGE
PREFACE BY CLOUGH WILLIAMS-ELLIS, F.R.I.B.A., M.T.P.I.	v
FOREWORD	vii
INTRODUCTION	11

ITINERARIES:—

1. THE SHAKESPEARE COUNTRY	21
2. THE COTSWOLDS	33
3. NORTH WALES	43
4. UNSPOILT DORSET	55
5. THE WYE VALLEY	66
6. "LITTLE ENGLAND BEYOND WALES "—THE PEMBROKESHIRE COAST	78
7. SMUGGLERS' COAST—THE LIZARD PENINSULA	89
8. FROM DUNKERY TO TINTAGEL	101
9. ENGLISH LAKELAND	113
10. THE YORKSHIRE COAST	125
11. THE PEAK DISTRICT	137
12. THE PILGRIMS' WAY	150

APPENDICES:—

(a) USEFUL ADDRESSES	168
(b) A FEW BOOKS TO READ	175

INTRODUCTION

Glory to your feet—
Albanian road greeting.

THE real fun of hiking can only be got by one who is content to travel simply. To each one of us there comes a time when we are tired of towns. We want a simpler way of life for a change. We want to go wandering about the woods, fields, hills, and along the sea-coast, free from our jobs, our cares, and the domination of the clock.

At the present time there is a more widespread appreciation of Britain's natural beauty and of historic buildings than ever before. More and more city dwellers desire to take their holidays amidst unspoiled country scenes. Holidays with pay, and the ever-increasing membership—already running into hundreds of thousands—of various clubs and associations, such as the Youth Hostels Association, the Ramblers' Association, the Camping Club of Great Britain, the Cyclists' Touring Club, etc., are cheering signs of the times.

I " discovered " England during the war. Previously I had wandered about in most parts of the world, neglecting my own land. Then, while serving in the R.A.F., stationed as I was in various parts of Britain, I found great joy during my periods of leave and leisure time in exploring a countryside which was an astounding revelation to me, with its superb beauty and its fascinating historic interest. After leaving the Service, I carried on with my rambles. This book is the result.

No claim is made that the routes detailed are the " best " ones—that, after all, is a matter of personal opinion—but they are representative of various types of scenery in different parts of England and Wales. Thus you can have your choice of hills and mountains, moor and fell, downland and wolds, lakes and coastland, heath and forest—all forming part of that fascinating jigsaw, the English countryside.

LET'S GO HIKING

Obviously seasoned ramblers hardly require a book of this nature, which is primarily meant to assist persons who are less knowledgeable to derive the most benefit from a health-giving, interesting, and enjoyable walking-holiday. Nor is it intended for those who wish to cover " record " distances, regardless of the surrounding countryside and its interests.

About our weather

Most hikers want sunshine during their holidays rather than rain. Here are a few facts about our weather: the best month for sunshine is generally June, but in the south there is not much to choose between May, June and July. The warmest month is usually July; August scores in West Wales and around the Cornish coast. Sussex and the Isle of Wight are the sunniest parts of Britain. April is the driest month, with Kent, Essex and the Fenlands the driest spots. Snowdonia is the wettest part of Britain (more than 200 ins.), with the Lake District taking second place (up to 180 ins.). The Devon-Cornish uplands have more than 60 ins.

Choosing your holiday and its cost

At the head of each itinerary I give a brief description of its main attractions and features. The choice, then, and it is a varied one, rests with you. Your expenses will vary according to your tastes, but five pounds should amply cover the cost of a seven-day walking tour, apart from your rail fare. You can secure a reduction in your rail fare, if you are a member of one of the associations—the Ramblers' Association, the Youth Hostels Association, etc.—for they provide their members with " Point to point " vouchers, enabling them to secure concessions on the railways (this privilege is now being negotiated).

Planning your tour

The itineraries given in this book are aimed at *helping* you make up your mind, rather than *making* it up for you, surely the better service of the two; and so the walking tours which

INTRODUCTION 13

you will read here are not to be followed slavishly, but are meant to entice you, and provide sufficient information to help you. The fun of hiking, as in all travel, consists largely in chance encounters and unpremeditated moves; so leave part of the details of your holiday in the hands of Fate. Too much precision is a mistake.

The general plan I have adopted, based on my own experience, is to walk between 80 and 100 miles in the seven days. Usually another two days are required to reach the starting-point and returning home from the terminal. These two days include exploration of both starting and finishing places, which often are of interest. *Do not try to cover too much ground.* Exhaustion is not the best way to enjoy a tour. If you are at all out of condition make the first day or two short distances. Start early—the best part of the day anyhow—and finish early enough to secure accommodation. It's not much fun searching for a bed late in the evening when you are probably tired and hungry. Take a bus (if available) should you feel " done up ", and don't necessarily exhaust a tour in one holiday, but leave some delightful country for future tours. If you have a fortnight's holiday I suggest you take rest days at favoured spots *en route*, making rambles in the surrounding countryside. Twelve to fifteen miles a day is a good average to aim at, for this allows you time for the subsidiary pleasures of walking, such as visiting historic buildings, resting and reading, talking to the country-folk, and so on. Remember also that in " difficult " country your speed is necessarily reduced. For practical reasons, I have tried, as far as possible, to end each day's walk in a town or big village, where it is easier to find accommodation.

Hiking alone, or with a party

My instincts are those of a solitary and so I travel alone, but I pick up acquaintances everywhere and chance companionship is the best of all. If, however, you are diffident on this point, or prefer the social aspects of company, then make sure your companion or companions have compatible tastes in all respects. On one occasion I made a tour along the Roman

Wall in company—but never again. My friend would insist on walking ahead and making the pace all the time.

The Ramblers'. Association have many local clubs, and they provide facilities for walking in company.

Clothes and footwear

Unsuitable clothes and footwear can ruin a holiday—especially footwear. I wear a good, strong pair of boots or shoes—and keep them well dubbined. There should be room for the toes to move, but the heel should not slip, or blisters will result. See that your footwear is properly soled and heeled before setting out. By the way, remember not to put wet boots too close to a fire to dry, as the heat will crack the leather and spoil them.

Look after your feet, especially the first day or two of a tour. Wash them once a day and sprinkle them with boracic powder. Woollen socks are best, for they keep your feet ventilated. Rubbing soap inside the socks often helps personal comfort. Have a clean pair of socks to change into for the evening; and I also carry a pair of light shoes which helps one's feet to relax.

With clothing, never forget the fickleness of the British climate. Shorts are the best hiking wear for men, and often with girls, although with the latter, divided skirts have aesthetic advantages! Plus fours are handy, and riding breeches with leggings are best if the country is rough. I personally wear flannel trousers, although they are uncomfortable if they get wet round the knees and ankles.

For the rest, I like a lumber-jacket, a sleeveless pullover (in case it gets chilly), my usual underwear, a rambler's cape, and a beret (although I prefer to walk bare-headed).

Equipment

The rucksack is the most important item, and I strongly recommend the type with metal frame and three pockets. Don't skimp on this piece of equipment, for second only to bad footwear, false economy on this item can spoil your

INTRODUCTION

holiday. "Travel light" is the golden rule after that. If you are camping out, read the handbook of the Camping Club of Great Britain, which has a detailed chapter on "Pedestrian Camping".

Other recommended items of equipment are—a pocket torch, a compass (essential for moorland tours), a pocket First-Aid outfit and a reserve ration of chocolate.

Packing the rucksack

There is a proper way of packing a rucksack. Put the things which you will want last at the bottom—night attire, spare clothing, iron rations, etc.—and soap, towel, sandwiches, etc., at the top where they can be reached without disturbing everything. Maps, hat, books, camera should be placed in the outer pockets. Mackintosh or cape can be strapped on top so that it is not necessary to delve inside if it rains.

To prevent the contents of pack rolling together into an untidy heap I advise having a number of small cotton or waterproof bags and stowing the various items in them. Towel, washing and shaving kit will go in one: clean clothing in another: perishable foods such as bread, meat and cereals can also be kept in bags. A tin box similar in size to a half-size biscuit tin or slightly smaller is useful for holding perishable foods. Containers of bakelite or aluminium will hold jam, sugar, tea, etc., but if you like, ordinary tins with tight-fitting lids will do.

Maps

There is only one kind of map which I would ever recommend to the hiker—the one-inch Ordnance Survey maps. An entirely new map, the two-and-a-half inch, is in course of preparation. This larger scale is ideal for ramblers and others interested in a close study of the countryside. Any smaller scale than one-inch is useless, for paths are not shown. The information given you in this book is based on the assumption that you carry one-inch Ordnance maps of the area covered in your itinerary. In fact, this book's job is partly intended to supplement the map. Make yourself familiar with the conventional signs used on maps for various landmarks, as they help greatly in finding your way. Contour lines show altitude. If you are shaky on map-reading, get practice before you start on a tour. The Ramblers' Association sell a useful little publication on "Map Reading", priced 1s. 6d.

Stanfords, Long Acre, London, W.C.2, are the official agents for the sale of Ordnance Survey maps. But your local bookseller, the Y.H.A., the Ramblers' Association, etc., can obtain any map required. These maps cost 2s. for the paper edition, 3s. for the linen-backed edition, and 5s. for the dissected edition. It is not always possible to obtain copies, however, of all the areas in the linen-backed editions. It is not difficult to mount a paper map yourself.

At the present time the Ordnance Survey are bringing out a new series of one-inch maps—the "New Popular Edition"—which, in due course, will supplant the existing "Popular Edition". So far only Southern England has been dealt with. In the list of maps given at the head of each itinerary, I have indicated the "New Popular Edition" numbers by (N.P.). Index sheets for both editions can be obtained at 2d. each from Stanfords.

Remember that the marking of a path on an Ordnance map does not necessarily mean that a right-of-way exists. The same thing applies to mention of paths in this book.

Carry a compass and learn how to use it. It is essential in moorland country, where fogs and sudden mists often descend; otherwise you may well get "lost".

Books

Your personal interests will decide what books you should carry. Many guide books are at present out of print. Locally, however, you can usually buy small guides that help you in seeing interesting things. Your local public library may have books dealing with the country you are going to visit, and a perusal of these, both before and after your holiday, can add to its enjoyment. The titles of a few recommended books are given in Appendix B.

INTRODUCTION

In addition, I like to carry a long classic with me. I read through Borrow's *Bible in Spain* on my Cotswolds tour, and Thackeray's *Henry Esmond* on the Yorkshire Coast.

Hobbies

Even a slight knowledge of such subjects as geology, natural history, architecture or archaeology adds much to the enjoyment of a walking tour. The naturalist in particular has unlimited opportunities of observing the habits of the birds and other wild life which may be encountered. Wild flowers and trees can provide many thrills. The photographer has great moments, and the historically-minded will find memorials of the past everywhere. Garden lovers should write to the Queen's Institute of District Nursing, 57 Lower Belgrave Street, London, S.W.1, for a list of famous private gardens that are open to the public at certain times during the summer months. Perhaps one or more of these lovely English gardens may lie on your route.

Accommodation

This can range from camping out to spending the night in a first-class hotel. Camping out solves a lot of troubles, for accommodation can otherwise be a problem, especially during the popular holiday months, June to September. Outside of main centres I have sometimes found accommodation on farms and in cottages. Youth hostels are the ideal for most hikers, but you must be a member of the Association. Their current list of hostels open will assist you in planning your stopping-places for the night. New hostels are constantly being opened, while some are closed down. Make certain on this point.

Hostels are open to persons of all ages. Members can cook their own meals or buy food at reasonable prices. Membership costs from one to seven shillings—and the benefits are well worth this subscription. There is a friendly atmosphere to be found in youth hostels, and one gains enjoyable memories of cheery evenings spent round the common-room fire.

The Camping Club of Great Britain provides its members with a list of camping-grounds. You can usually, however, find camping places, but get the owner's permission first. And leave the site tidy when you leave, also extinguishing all fires.

Where may one walk?

Many ramblers have only vague ideas about their rights as wayfarers, and imagine they can wander anywhere at will. On agricultural and cultivated land one is confined to rights-of-way—roads, lanes, and paths. If you stray from these you are trespassing, and although many owners are civil and obliging, others may order you off their land and can use " necessary force " if you refuse. You are not obliged to go back the way you came, but must be allowed to make for the nearest public right-of-way. Trespass incurs no legal penalty so long as no damage is committed; politeness is your best weapon in difficult cases.

It is an offence for a person to set a dog at a trespasser. " Trespassers will be prosecuted " is a meaningless threat. " Private Road " may be misleading. Coastguard paths and towing paths are not necessarily open to the public. Most paths shown on the Ordnance maps are public, and often many others. Owners often have legal rights over mountains, moorlands and uncultivated land.

This important subject of access to the countryside is fully dealt with in a booklet called *Right of Way*, published by the Ramblers' Association (post free, 10*d*.). All ramblers are advised in their own interest to support this organisation, whose avowed objects are: " To protect the interest of ramblers, and to maintain their rights and privileges; to foster a greater love, use and knowledge of the countryside; to secure travel facilities and to obtain public access to uncultivated mountains and moorlands."

Finally

Don't try to break records.
Don't dread an occasional night in the open.

INTRODUCTION

Do not fail to greet passers-by in the country, if only with a cheerful grin.
Keep to the path.
Close and secure all gates.
Avoid causing damage.
Pick flowers sparingly.
On roads, use the sidewalk.
Avoid starting fires.
Respect and be respected.
Be cheerful and interested in everything.
Do not bother too much about your inside—or the troubles of the outer world, for the time being.
And, finally, don't forget the old saying:

> " But while I plan and plan, my hair
> Is grey before I know it."

So, get " cracking ", and

LET'S GO HIKING. . . .

KEY TO MAPS

Main Tour on Road ——————

Main Tour over footpaths
or across country ....

Main Tour crosses main road ≠

Main Tour crosses secondary road ≠

Points of interest mentioned
specially in text ▲

Rivers ～～～

Town at which the hiker stays
the night. ☐

1. THE SHAKESPEARE COUNTRY

Best loved and most visited place of pilgrimage for the English-speaking race is the little town of Stratford on Avon, for here was born, lived, and died William Shakespeare, England's most illustrious son. After Stratford itself the country around is most alluring to those wishing to seek out the haunts of Shakespeare. It is a sweet and pleasant corner of England, with its many charming old-world villages, ancient churches, and picturesque Elizabethan manor-houses and country homes—all set in a typical English scene.

Summary of distances

1. STRATFORD ON AVON Tour of town	2 miles
2. One-day tour, via Charlecote and Snitterfield, returning to STRATFORD	13 ,,
3. Two-day tour, via Long Marston and Pepworth to MICKLETON, and via	13 ,
4. Quinton and Clifford Chambers to STRATFORD ON AVON	12 ,,
5. Three-day tour, via Wilmcote and Aston Cantlow to ALCESTER, and via	12 ,,
6. Exhall, Wixford and Broom to BIDFORD, and via	11 ,,
7. Hillborough and Temple Grafton to STRATFORD ON AVON	10 ,,
Total Distance	73 ,,

Train travel

Arrive and depart : Stratford on Avon Station. G.W.R. and L.M.S.

Bus travel
 Midland Red Omnibus Co., Ltd.
 Stratford Blue Motor Services, Ltd.

Maps
 One-inch Ordnance Survey, sheet 82.

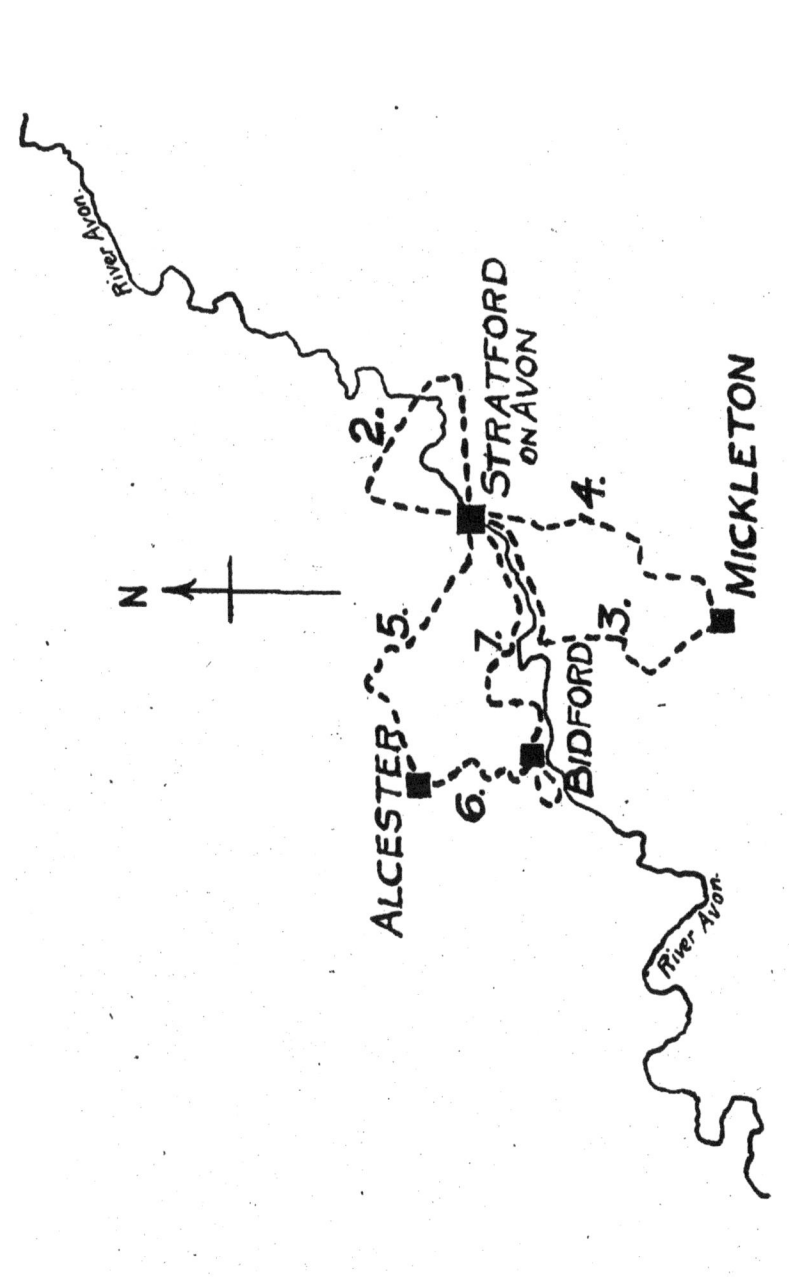

FIRST DAY

From Great Western Railway Station, proceed along Station Road and Greenhill Street to the American Fountain, given by G. W. Childs, of Philadelphia, as a tribute to Shakespeare, and erected in 1887 to commemorate Queen Victoria's Jubilee. Turn left into Windsor Street, then right into Henley Street. On the left is Shakespeare's birthplace (admission—fee). Beyond is the Public Library. At the traffic island turn right into High Street. On the right is Harvard House, named after the founder of the famous American University (admission—fee). Across the road on the next corner is the Town Hall, dedicated by David Garrick in 1769 to the memory of Shakespeare. On the next corner is Nash's House and New Place Museum, with gardens of the original building, where the playwright lived after his return from London, still flowering and open to visitors. Opposite on the left are the ancient Guild Chapel and Grammar School (admission only out of school hours—fee). Continuing along Church Street, Mason Croft—at one time the home of the famous novelist Marie Corelli—is on the right.

At the next cross-roads turn left through Old Town, and so reach Holy Trinity Church, where Shakespeare is buried. (Those who enter Stratford on Avon by the L.M.S. Station arrive at the church via New Street, then right into College Lane.) Return to Old Town and take the first on the right—Southern Lane—and so pass the Memorial Theatre, adjoining which is the Shakespeare Library and Picture Gallery. At the end of the street turn right to view the fifteenth-century Clopton Bridge, after which return to town via Bridge Street.

Distance 2 miles.

SECOND DAY

Leave Stratford on Avon by crossing Clopton Bridge, and then turn left alongside the River Avon, but take the first turning on the right and so avoid the main road. Loxley

THE SHAKESPEARE COUNTRY

Lane climbs Alveston Hill. Just beyond the top take a path to the left, that dips to cross a stream and, 1½ miles farther, by pond, turn left to cross main road and then the River Dene. Charlecote Park, the imposing Elizabethan home of the Lucy family, is to be seen on the left. Pass the church and skirt the park—the reputed scene of the poaching episode of the youthful Shakespeare—and so cross the Avon into Hampton Lucy. See the cathedral-like church, but return to fork by bridge, where turn left up hill and, ½ mile on, bear left. At next junction keep right and then cross main Stratford–Warwick road. Just over ¼ mile on, take footpath to left, come out on the road, turn left and then right for Snitterfield. A black-and-white cottage near where the village is entered was the home of Richard Shakespeare, William's grandfather, who rented it from Robert Arden, father of Mary, the mother of the playwright. Pass the old church, hidden away in the trees, and take first turn on left and strike across by footpath to right. At end, across road, follow road going southward. This leads to Stratford, but a footpath on the right (¾ mile), goes more directly and pleasantly past Welcombe—now an hotel, but one time home of Robert Phillips, who erected obelisk on hill on left, as a memorial to his brother, Mark. This way passes by The Dingles—a deep ravine, which was probably a prehistoric earthwork.

STRATFORD is entered by the Warwick Road.

Distance 13 miles.

THIRD DAY

By crossing the river and following the footpath southwards along its bank, a fine view of the Memorial Theatre is obtained. This path passes under two railway bridges and eventually comes out on a road ¾ mile east of Weston on Avon, a village much favoured by artists. Continuing past the church, another footpath leaves the river after a short distance and turns to Welford. Here turn southward and climb by the road over Rumer Hill to Long Marston, the " Dancing Marston " of the rhyme about the eight villages, noted for its Morris dances.

"King's Lodge" housed Charles II for one night during his flight, disguised as a servant, after the Battle of Worcester in 1651. Take the road north of this house, that is, the first on the right, cross the brook and then turn left for "Piping" Pebworth, with its church peeping above the trees on the hilltop, and around which is a cluster of charming old cottages. Turn south-eastward for Broad Marston, pass under the railway and ascend to MICKLETON—which, strictly speaking, is outside of the Shakespeare Country, but is a delightful unspoiled Cotswold village.

Distance 13 miles

FOURTH DAY

Leave by the main Stratford road, but take first turn on right towards the rising ground, and after a mile on this road turn left to climb Meon Hill. It is crowned by an encampment, and from it a very extensive view is obtained—including the Avon Valley, the Cotswolds, Edgehill and, on a very clear day, the Clee Hills and the Wrekin. Descend to the village lying on the Stratford side—Quinton, divided into Upper and Lower. Keep right in the latter, pass the church and, at next fork, keep left. Then cross brook and take next turn on left, over Harbour Hill and so to Preston on Stour. Do not cross the river, but skirt Alscot Park, lying beyond village, and so come by footpath to its neighbour, Atherstone on Stour. From the bend in the road by the church another footpath leads to Clifford Chambers. The fifteenth-century half-timbered rectory is claimed as the possible birthplace of William Shakespeare, as, in the year of his birth, when the plague was prevalent in Stratford, his parents had evacuated themselves to this delightful village. Michael Drayton, in whose company Shakespeare dined and wined just before his death, was a frequent visitor at the sixteenth-century manor-house, which, unfortunately, was burnt in 1918. The main road leads back to STRATFORD ON AVON.

Distance 12 miles.

FIFTH DAY

From the Alcester road, near its junction with Station Road, is a footpath leading to Shottery. To see Ann Hathaway's cottage, turn right by the inn, then left, and cross the brook, beyond which, on the left, lies the home of Shakespeare's wife. Farther up the lane is Hathaway Farm, a museum open to the public. Beyond, follow the footpath that leads on to the main Stratford–Alcester road. Cross this and traverse the slight ridge for about 1½ miles, then turn right for Wilmcote, where, among unattractive brick cottages, is a long half-timbered building with dormer windows—the home of Mary Arden, William Shakespeare's mother. Follow straight through village. One mile beyond at road junction turn right to Aston Cantlow. Here, it is reputed, Mary Arden was married to John Shakespeare. There are fragments of a Norman castle, excavated by a recent vicar of the village. Return from village to road junction just south of it and turn right by a road that just skirts the River Alne and then make for Haselor. The modest fourteenth-century church stands apart on a hill and from there a pleasant prospect is seen. Continue straight on by the road that gradually approaches the river and then, from Oversley Green, cross it into ALCESTER, an old market town of Roman origin, where Malt Mill Lane, with its line of timbered cottages, is worth a visit.

Distance 12 miles.

SIXTH DAY

Return to Oversley Green, turn right, then left, climb Primrose Hill, skirt Oversley Wood and so come to " Dodging " Exhall, a pretty out-of-the-way village, from the churchyard of which a good view of the Avon Valley is obtained. Southwestward lies " Papist " Wixford, a good angling haunt, being by the River Arrow. It stands on Ickneild Street, an ancient road, which now follow southward for ¾ mile, then turn left to visit " Beggarly " Broom. One street leads down to the river, there turn left, and, a few yards on, left again to return by a parallel street. From this turn right, cross the railway and so come to "Drunken" Bidford, past its eight-arched fifteenth-century bridge, buttressed on one side only. An Elizabethan house by the church was formerly the Falcon Inn, the reputed scene of the young Shakespeare's carousals. In 1925 the site of a sixth-century pre-Christian cemetery was excavated nearby and the relics transferred to New Place Museum at Stratford. Cross the bridge and take footpath on right, which leads to Marcliff. Leaving the village on the left, a path goes round under the hill and in a mile comes to a charming scene, with a mill seen across the weir. Inland from here a footpath leads steeply up to Cleeve Prior, a delightful spot, clustering round its old grey church with its lofty tower. By the inn turn left and go by road back through Marcliff and, by turning left at cross-roads ½ mile on, to BIDFORD.

Distance 11 miles.

SEVENTH DAY

Leaving the main road by the church and turning off to the right, a footpath near the river leads to "Haunted" Hillborough, a small hamlet with a Tudor manor-house and also a twelfth-century stone circular dovecot standing by a pond in the meadow. Turning north, away from the river, join the road, cross the railway and take next turn on left, beyond which bear right for Temple (" Hungry ") Grafton, the eighth of the doggerel villages and traditionally the scene of Shakespeare's marriage. Turn right and, by inn at next cross-roads, turn right again for Binton. The west window of the church is a memorial to Captain Scott and depicts incidents of his Antarctic explorations. The roads on either side of the church will lead to the main road, along which turn left and take the first on the right for Luddington. This village also claims to be the scene of the poet's wedding to Ann Hathaway. The road, or the footpath by the river, may be followed back to STRATFORD.

Distance 10 miles.

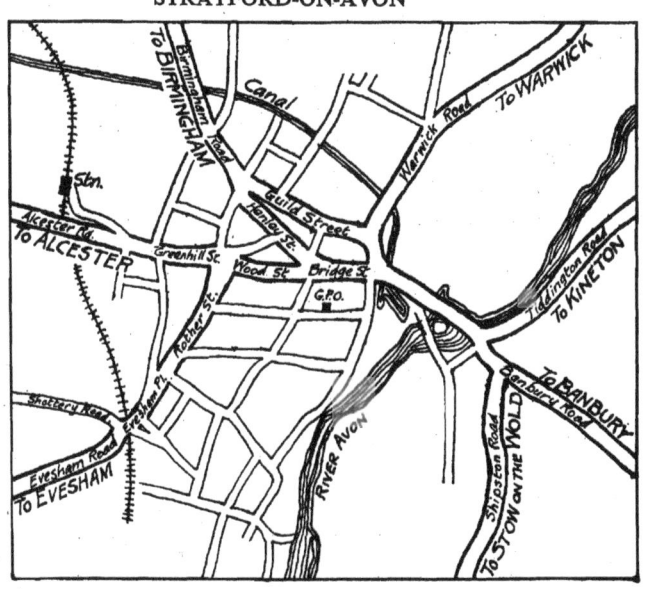

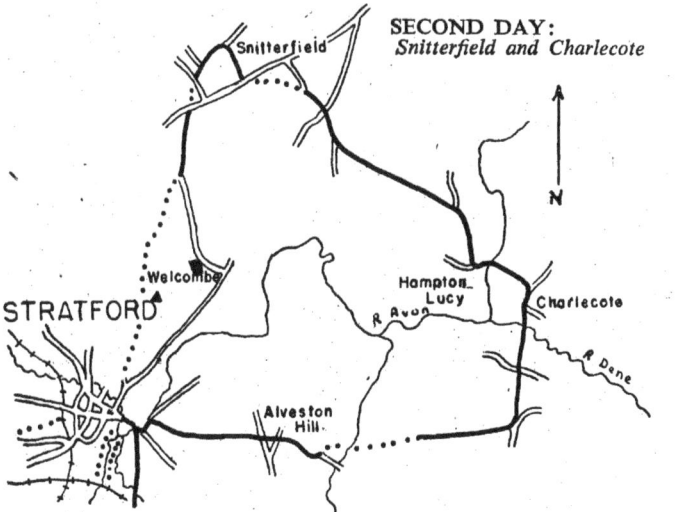

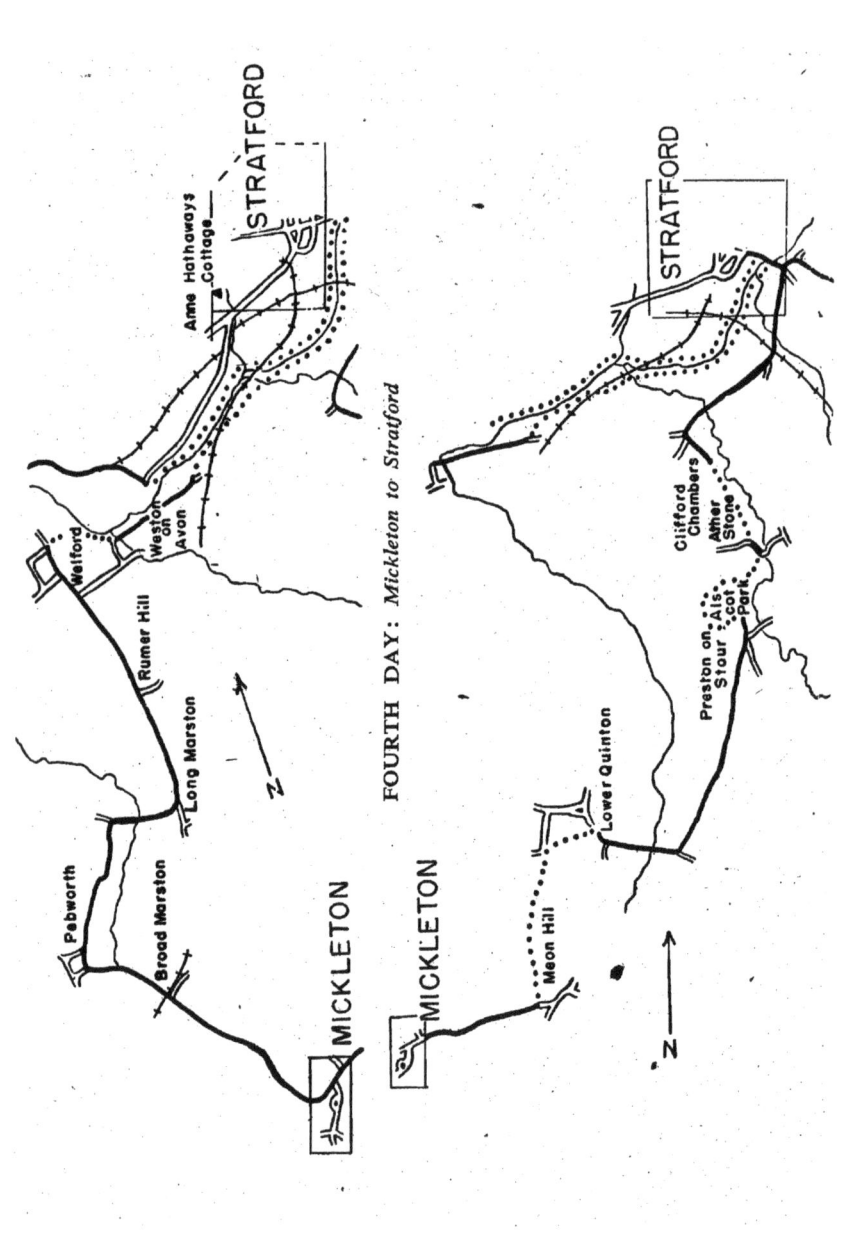

FOURTH DAY: *Mickleton to Stratford*

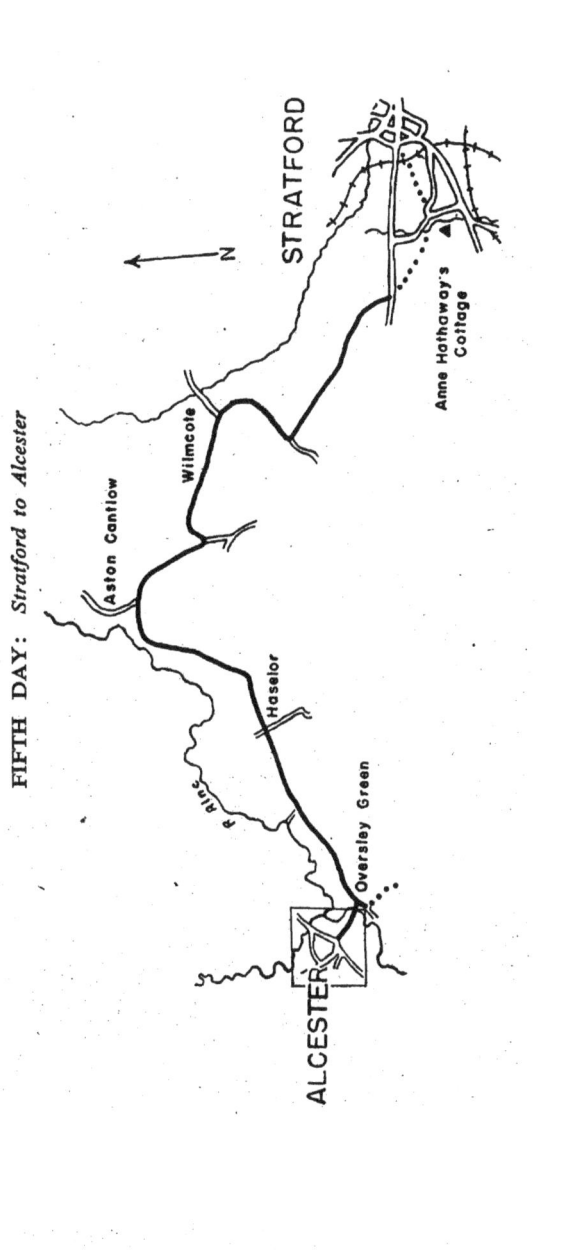

FIFTH DAY: *Stratford to Alcester*

SIXTH DAY: *Alcester to Bidford*

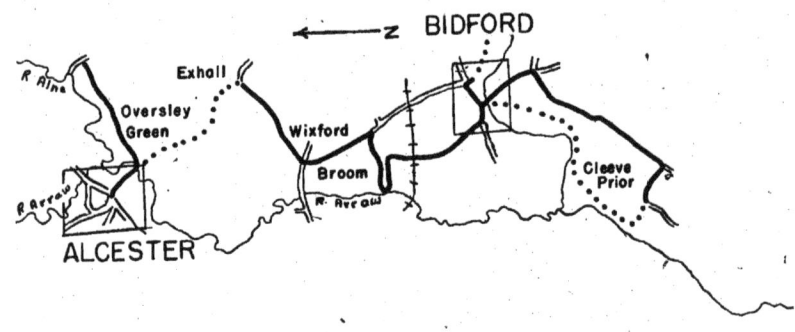

SEVENTH DAY: *Bidford to Stratford*

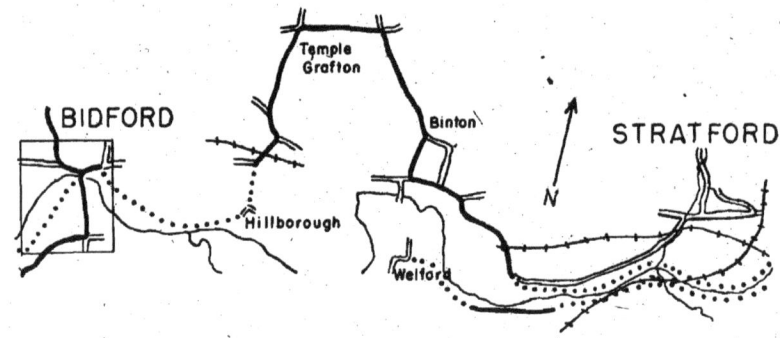

2. THE COTSWOLDS

My first walking tour in England was the one I now describe in the Cotswolds. It was in the month of June, and I had glorious weather. That week remains as one of my fondest and happiest memories—memories of mellow villages, ancient churches, historic wool towns, gently flowing streams, and lovely scenery. The scenery is of its kind hardly to be excelled. Even the names of some of the places I visited—Chipping Campden, Moreton-in-Marsh, Stow-on-the-Wold, Bourton-on-the-Water—seem to hold the essence of England's past. All these places flourished in the great wool days.

Summary of Distances
1. CHELTENHAM TO WINCHCOMBE . . 9 miles
2. BROADWAY . . . . . . 13 ,,
3. By Chipping Campden, Bourton-on-the-Hill, to MORETON-IN-MARSH . . . . 12 ,,
4. STOW-ON-THE-WOLD . . . . 11 ,,
5. By Bourton-on-the-Water to NORTHLEACH . 12 ,,
6. BIBURY . . . . . . 14 ,,
7. By Quenington to CIRENCESTER . . 13 ,,

    Total Distance . . . . . 84 ,,

Train travel
Cheltenham and Cirencester. G.W.R.

Bus travel
Midland Red Motor Omnibus Co., Ltd.
City of Oxford Motor Services, Ltd.
Bristol Tramways.

Maps
One-inch Ordnance Survey, sheets 93, 104.

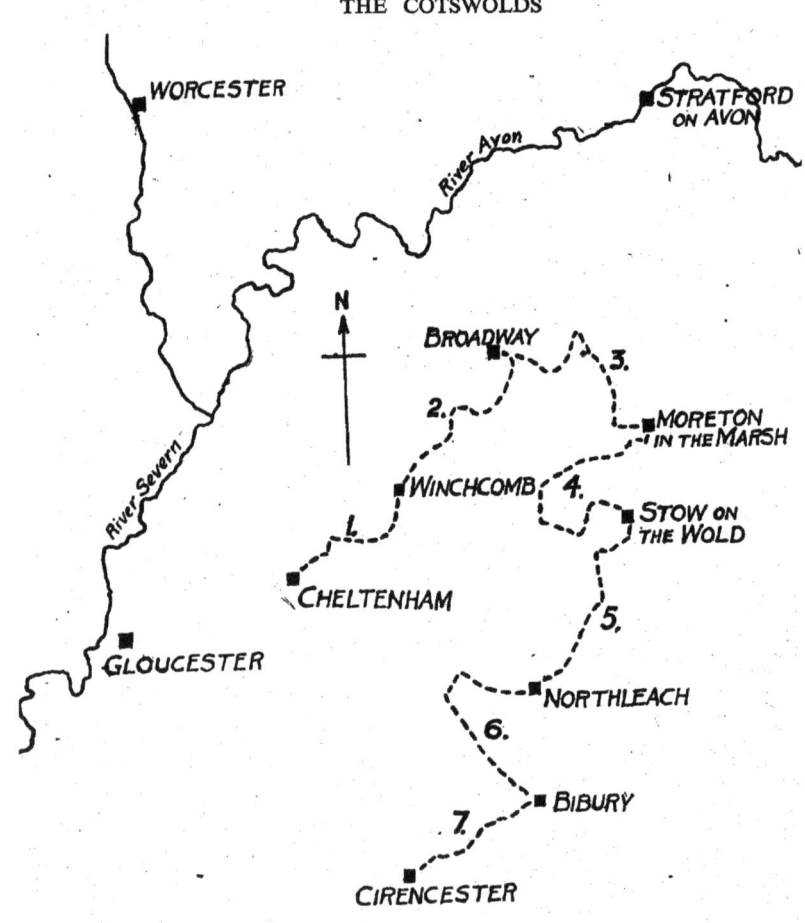

FIRST DAY

From Cheltenham walk or take a bus through the suburb of Prestbury to Southam. By the bus-passenger shelter take the path up the hillside to Huddlestone Table—a slab of rock marking the spot where Kenulph, King of Mercia, parted company with Cuthred, King of Kent, Sired of the East Saxons and others after the dedication of St. Peter's Abbey at Winchcombe in 798. Above is an ancient British camp, and having attained the ridge turn right along a path which leads to the highest point of the Cotswolds (1,076 ft.). At the junction of paths turn left and proceed eastward to Wontley Farm, where turn left in a north-easterly direction. About a mile on is Belas Knap, a Neolithic long-barrow, the scene in 1863 of the discovery of thirty-eight skeletons. From here a charming view is obtained of Sudeley Castle and Winchcombe. Descend through or skirt wood in the direction of the former, and strike a footpath from Wadfield Farm, which joins a road on the outskirts of Winchcombe.

Distance 9 miles.

SECOND DAY

Leave Winchcombe by Broadway road and just after passing over River Isbourne turn right (avoid road on right immediately over bridge). The lane leading N.E. develops into a footpath and leads over the foot of the hill to Hailes, where there are interesting remains of a Cistercian abbey—now the property of the National Trust. Admission to abbey and museum 6*d*. From the church a footpath goes northward to Didbrook, where turn right, pass church and turn left at road junction for Stanway. Pass war memorial at cross-roads and by the church (note gatehouse, attributed to Inigo Jones) to the residence of the Earl of Wemyss and March, and the medieval tithe barn. Continue along road with Cotswolds on right to Stanton, an enchanting village. Just south of the church a lane leads over the hill to Snowshill. The road to

36   LET'S GO HIKING

left of church leads to Broadway, but by turning up the hill for ½ mile and then turning left, and again left ¾ mile farther, a walk along the ridge brings you to the top of Broadway Hill, whence the main road leads down to BROADWAY, the village beloved of American tourists. Alternatively there are paths down the hill before the road is reached.

Distance 13 miles.

THIRD DAY

Either ascend Broadway Hill and take first turn on left, or go north from centre of village to Willersey, but follow on at Cross-roads near entrance and ascend Long Hill. Two and a quarter miles on, turn right to Chipping Campden, one of the historic wool towns. Continue southward and up the hill by a road leading alongside Northwick Park (on left) to Blockley, set in a fold of the hills. Straight through the village the road leads to Bourton Woods. By keeping left Bourton-on-the-Hill is gained. Continue eastward for 2 miles to MORETON-IN-MARSH, a charming Cotswold market town.

Distance 12 miles.

FOURTH DAY

Leave Moreton by the Stow road and ¼ mile out turn right by track and footpath that leads south-westwards to Longborough. At ¼ mile westwards are cross-roads. Continue straight ahead, cross main road and proceed to Condicote, passing Eubury Camp—an ancient encampment on right as road commences to climb to village. Proceed southward, making for highest point, crossing main road *en route*. From summit descend to next road and turn left to Lower Swell, lying in a district abounding in prehistoric remains. The old church was built over the site of a Roman crematorium. Upper Swell, an equally picturesque village, lies along the road northward, or it may be reached by the path alongside the River Dikler. Eastward of the village a by-road leaves the

THE COTSWOLDS 37

main road and continues alongside the river. By the mill turn right at main road and follow this and up hill to STOW-ON-THE-WOLD, an old greystone town which figured prominently in the Civil War in 1646.
Distance 11 miles.

FIFTH DAY

Take the road southward. By the Farmers' Arms Inn the road forks and on the right there is a track which goes westward down to the river, beyond which take road to left and then 1,000 yards on turn right to the picturesquely situated village of Upper Slaughter. Its companion, Lower Slaughter, to the south-east, is much frequented by artists. From the church in the latter place, to the southward, a footpath continues on to the main road, which follow for a short distance to the right and then take first turn on left for Bourton-on-the-Water, one of the most beautiful of Cotswold villages. From it a delightful rustic footpath goes southward to Clapton, but by taking the road the ridge is attained and wider views obtained. Two miles from Bourton a junction of roads is reached (by the road route) and Clapton, remarkable for its tiny church, lies by road or footpath uphill to the eastward. (By path you come straight to the village.) From the road junction (previously mentioned) there is the choice of continuing ahead along the road or taking the footpath to the south-west. Both lead to Farmington. Westward from this delightful village is Norbury Camp, an ancient entrenchment with remains of a Roman villa and two Neolithic barrows nearby. Just over the hill south-westward lies NORTHLEACH.
Distance 12 miles.

SIXTH DAY

From the main cross-roads west of the town a footpath crosses the stream and runs alongside the copse and leads to Hampnett. Climbing beyond the village, strike left by the track on the north side of the long belt of trees and at the end of these take footpath to left, cross main road into road leading to Compton Abdale, another beauty spot. Turn left, southward, and up hill from here. After descending to River Coln, turn left at cross-roads. Proceed for 1 mile and on the right, on the edge of Chedworth Woods, are the famous remains of a Roman villa—one of the finest examples in England (National Trust, small fee). Continue to skirt woods to their eastern end, then cross road and drop down to Fossbridge. Cross main road near inn, and follow footpath towards Coln St. Denis, but continue southward alongside river, leaving village on its other bank. At Coln Rogers is the best preserved Saxon church in the Cotswolds. Continue to follow river path through Winson to road junction 1 mile beyond, where turn left and cross river into Ablington—the subject of Arthur Gibbs' *A Cotswold Village*. BIBURY is one of the prettiest villages in the county, and, some say, in the country.

Distance 14 miles.

SEVENTH DAY

See Arlington Row before proceeding downstream by road or river path to Coln St. Aldwyn, a charming village, the scene of the ministry of John Keble, the author of *The Christian Year*. Across the river is Quenington. At cross-roads just south of the bridge turn left to visit this village, which has a fine Norman church and the gatehouse of the vanished Knights Hospitallers' preceptory. By right turns, arrive back at cross-roads near bridge, where turn left and climb steadily to Akeman Street—which follows for $3\frac{1}{2}$ miles until the main road is reached, where turn left and so eventually arrive at CIRENCESTER—the capital of the Cotswolds, its main street lined with gabled and dormer Tudor houses. Two railways lead from this delightful place.

Distance 13 miles.

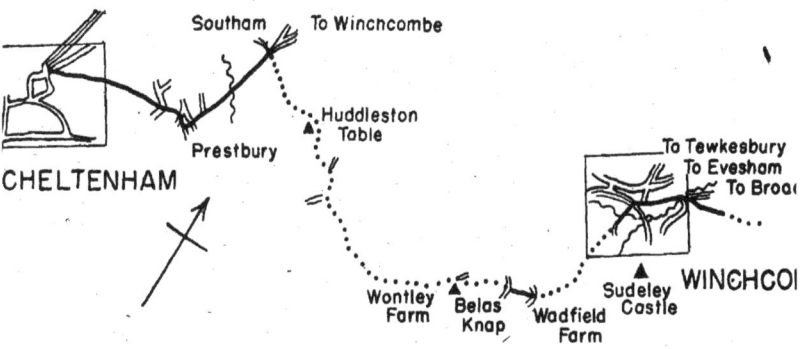

FIRST DAY: *Cheltenham to Winchcombe*

CHELTENHAM

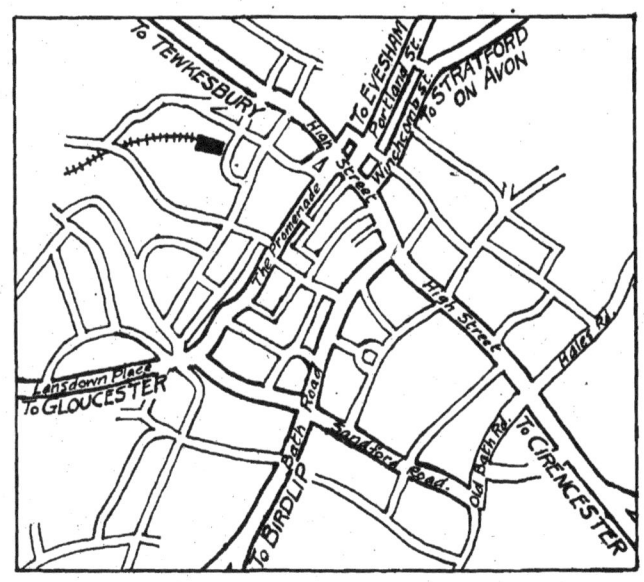

SECOND DAY: *Winchcombe to Broadway*

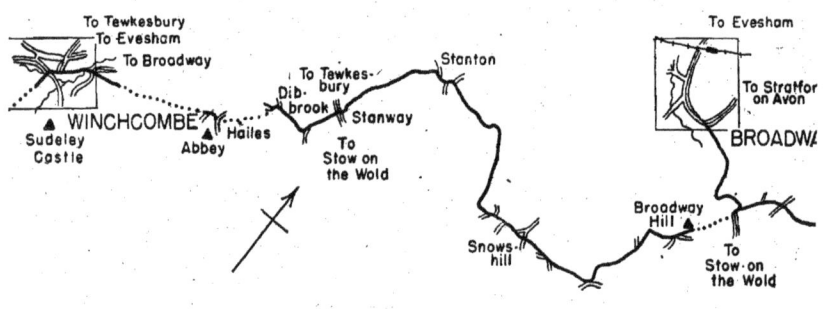

THIRD DAY: *Broadway to Moreton in Marsh*

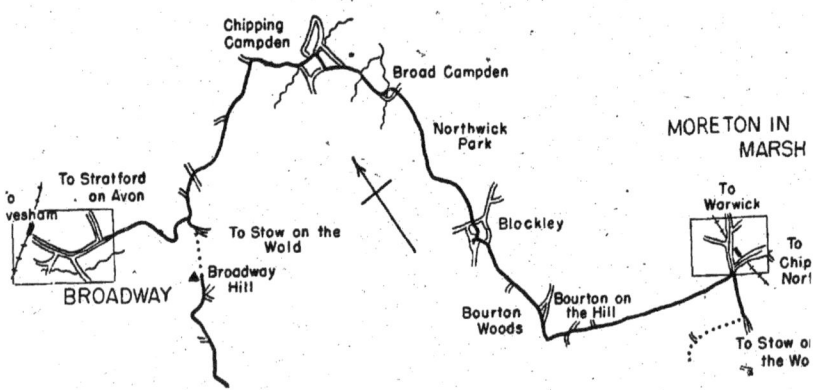

FOURTH DAY: *Moreton in Marsh to Stow on the Wold*

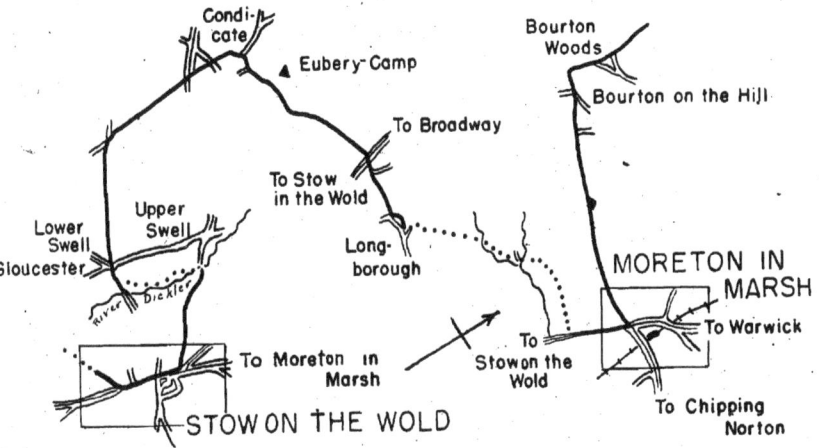

FIFTH DAY: *Stow on the Wold to Northleach*

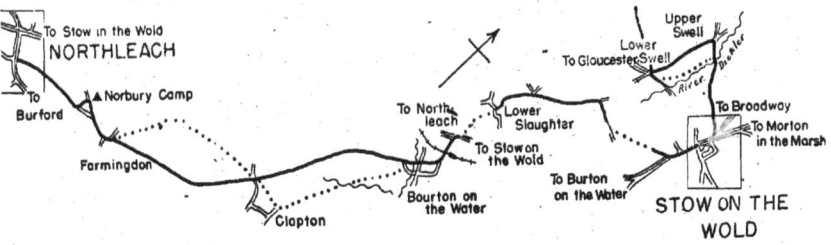

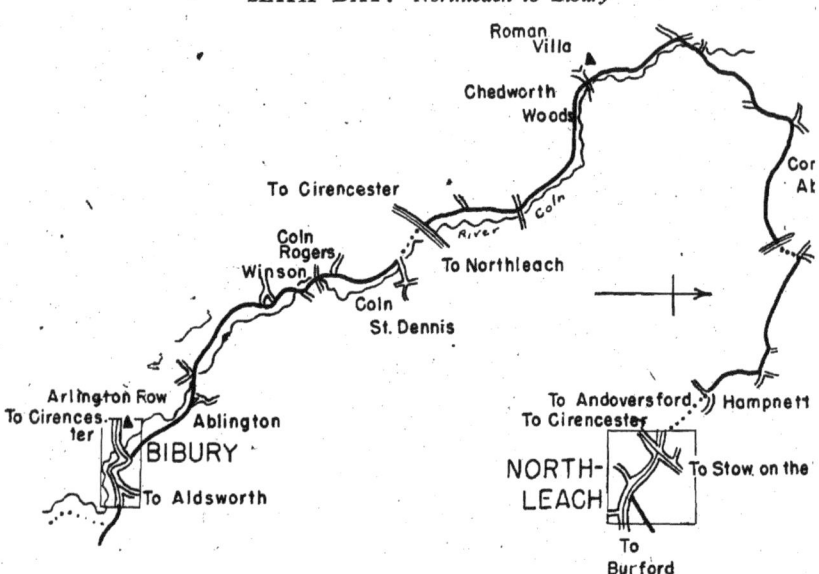

SIXTH DAY: *Northleach to Bibury*

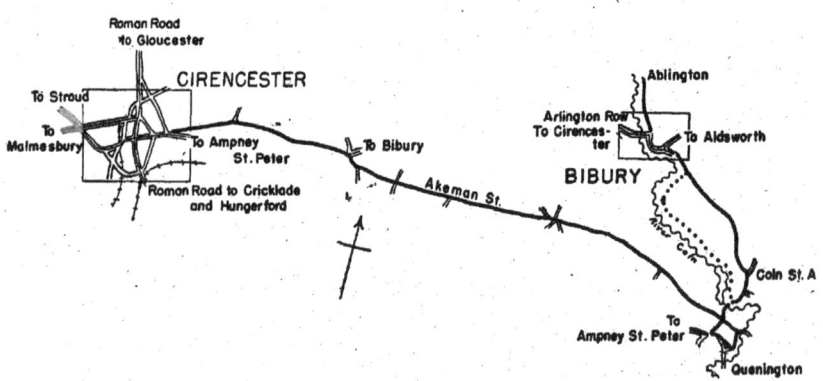

SEVENTH DAY: *Bibury to Cirencester*

3. NORTH WALES

Wales!—the name invariably brings to mind Snowdon, with its high peaks, spectacular ridges, and dark lakes—for to many people Snowdonia represents Wales. But actually North Wales is much more than Snowdon, attractive though it may be; one has only to think of the rolling green summits of the Clwyddian Hills, the purple heather-covered moors of Denbighshire, the rocky sea-coast from Llandudno westward, and the little-known Lleyn Peninsula, to realize this fact. Nor is North Wales just mountains—it is much more; lakes as fascinating as any in England's Lakeland, deep winding green valleys luxuriant with woodlands, and many historic old castles and towns. These are some of the reasons which yearly attract English people to the nearest " foreign " country within reach.

Summary of Distances

1. MOLD TO GYFFYLLIOG . . . . 13 miles
2. LLANSANNAN . . . . . . 12 ,,
3. LLANRWST . . . . . . 12 ,,
4. BETTWS-Y-COED . . . . . 10 ,,
5. FFESTINIOG . . . . . . 15 ,,
6. BEDDGELERT . . . . . . 15 ,,
7. LLANBERIS . . . . . . 15 ,,

    Total Distance . . . . . 92 ,,

Train travel
Mold and Caernarvon. L.M.S.

Bus travel
Crossville Motor Services, Ltd.

Maps
One-inch Ordnance Survey, sheets 41, 42, 43, 49, 50.

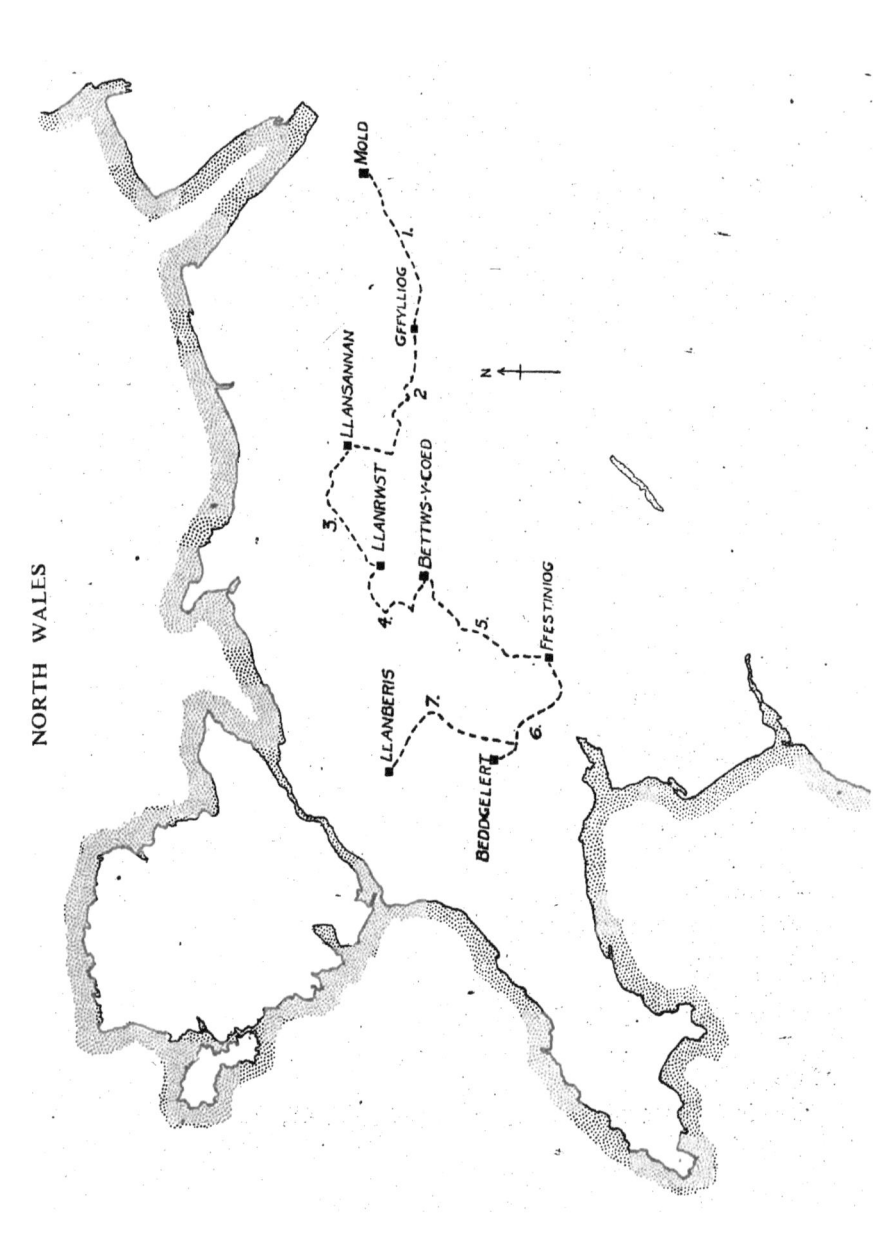

FIRST DAY

Mold is the nearest point to Moel Fammau, highest point of the Clwyddian Hills. Take old road to Ruthin past Jesuit College (formerly Mold Gaol). Climb uphill 2 miles. Road continues through wooded countryside past entrance to Colomendy Hall, home of Richard Wilson, the artist, to Loggerheads Inn. Loggerheads National Park, in the Alyn Valley, comprises forty acres of wooded limestone scenery. Continue along main road for $\frac{1}{2}$ mile to smithy, where road turns left, but the old road which you take continues straight on to the Pass of Bwlch-pen-Barras, 1,150 feet high. In autumn the heather in bloom makes a fine scene. (Those wishing to climb Moel Fammau (1,820 ft.), should turn right through gate and follow cart track to marshy hollow, where track can be seen continuing to summit. This is crowned by the ruins of the Jubilee Column erected in 1810 to commemorate the fiftieth year of George III's reign.) From the pass continue down road which descends to a plantation in the left, near Rhiwlas Farm. Leave road and descend hill on left, following path to gate leading into lane. Half a mile on road is reached, and, shortly after, Llanbedr, from which road or footpath can be taken to Ruthin. Ruthin or "Red Castle" (old church and castle) was besieged for three months by Parliamentary troops in Civil War. From town take road for 1 mile to alms-houses, where road divides, right-hand going to Hengoel in the valley of the Afon Clywedog. Where the road crosses river at Ty-brith, continue by old road along south bank of the river to GYFFYLLIOG.

Distance 13 miles.

SECOND DAY

Gyffylliog lies amidst the lovely and little-visited Denbigh Moors. To its south is the Mynydd Hiraethog, " the mountain of the long furze ", whose highest point is Mwdwl Eithin (1,742 ft.). The valley of the Afon Clywedog in which Gyffylliog lies is characteristic of the narrow, steep-sided valleys of the moorlands. Old carriage roads criss-cross the moors, and make for pleasant walking; but it is advisable to carry a compass in case of sudden mists. From Gyffylliog proceed up valley for 1½ miles, following old track running first along south bank of stream, then on north. Pass Bryn Ooyn to Rhyd Caled, cross old way running north and south and proceed along stream to point where it leaves Llyn Du, " the black lake ". Path curves round north end of lake, crosses road from Denbigh to Cerrig y Druidon, and then on to Pant y Maen. At ruined farm turn left along old road for ½ mile, then right for 1 mile to Llyn Bran. At head of lake the road from Bychau to Pentre Voelas is met. Turn left along it ¾ mile to Sportsman's Arms, nearly 1,500 feet up. Slightly north-west of inn is Gwylfa-Hiraethog (1,627 ft.). Bear north-west for almost a mile (no visible track) to Hafod-Dafydd. Short distance past bear west over Moel Bengam to Rhaiadr y Bedd in the Aled Valley. " The waterfall of the grave " is spectacular, plunging 75 feet over a black rock. From waterfall old roads lead along west bank of stream to LLANSANNAN.

Distance 12 miles.

THIRD DAY

From Llansannan walk ½ mile along road to Llanrwst. Where road makes a sharp turn to left a footpath continues north-west. It crosses a secondary road and proceeds over Pen y Mwdwl and then passes between Ffrith Bedwyn and Moel Unben, where old roads leads to Melai. Here turn right at motor road for 100 yards, then left at cross-roads, and continue to Llangerniew, in the Afon Gallen Valley. At inn turn left along road to Eglwys Fach for ¼ mile. Go along carriage-drive through Rhos y Maun park for 2 miles to Wenli. Continue to Ffrith-uchaf and cross-roads marked " Farmyard ", where you turn right along lane leading downhill between Pant-llin-Mawr and Pant-llin-Bach to Llanddoget. Main road continues downhill to Conway Valley and LLANRWST, but lane also goes past church in same direction.

NORTH WALES

Llanrwst, " The Church of Grwst ", has a delightful situation. It has a curious bridge which " if you put your back against the middle arch of one side and another person bumps the centre stone of the arch on the other side, a slight shake of the whole structure is said to be felt " (Baddeley). The church is attributed to Inigo Jones, and contains memorials of various Welsh princes. Half a mile away is Gwydir Castle (sixteenth century) which is open to the public.

Distance 12 miles.

FOURTH DAY

A short walk to allow time to visit many scenic haunts in this neighbourhood. From Llanrwst to Bettws-y-Coed by direct route is only 4 miles, but our route goes through some of the wildest corners of eastern Snowdonia. From Llanrwst take road by railway station, cross bridge over River Conway, and continue to Trefriw, " the town on the hillside "; the river is tidal up to this point, and steamers make the journey to Conway. Cross the Crafnant stream and take road on left up valley. Where it forks follow left branch to Llyn Crafnant, with the hills rising steeply on all sides. Road follows shore of the lake to Cynllwyd. A few yards on track bears left up hillside to top of ridge (960 ft.). Descend to Tal y Llyn Farm at head of Llyn Geirionydd. This is a region dotted with small lakes—some very tiny. Old road leads to Llyn Tyn y Mynydd and disused lead-mines. Turn sharp right along road to Ty Hyll Bridge, leading to main road from Capel Curig to Bettws y Coed. Turn left, and ½ mile downstream are the celebrated " Swallow Falls ". A mile farther on is the " Miner's Bridge ", where footpaths lead through the woods to a narrow road ending at BETTWS Y COED. Bettws y Coed, " The Chapel in the Wood ", is the centre of one of the most lovely districts in Britain. Situated at the junction of the Conway and Llugy Rivers, several days could be spent exploring such places as interest as: Fairy Glen, Conway Falls, Pandy Mill, Machno Falls, etc.

Distance 10 miles.

FIFTH DAY

Turn left at railway station, then right along main road. A short way along take lane (signposted " Elsi Lake "), leading uphill through woods and marked by posts. From crest of moor there is a fine view of Denbigh Moors and Moel Siabod. The lake can be seen in distance and track leads you there. From commemorative stone bear left to cottages, called " Hafod-las ", where path leads by several stiles to more cottages, beyond which lies the old Roman road—Sarn Helen (" the way of the legions "). Following in the footsteps of the ancient Romans, you pass Rhiw-ddolion and walk south-west to the Lledr Valley. This beautiful valley has been called " the Switzerland of Wales ". At Pont y Pant turn right along main road to Dolwyddelan, where Llewelyn the Great is said to have been born; the castle is a mile on. From village cross stream and railway to Pentre Bont, where lane proceeds up steep valley of Afon Cwm Penamnen to Gwyndy-newydd, surrounded on all sides by high peaks. Directly ahead is Foel Fra (1,920 ft.). From head of valley track leads straight up mountainside and over pass slightly below summit, then descending to Llyn Newydd (1,578 ft.). Where stream leaves south end of lake an old rail track from slate quarries leads down to outskirts of Blaenau Ffestiniog, where bus can be taken to Ffestiniog, 3 miles distant. To walk, take footpath starting from road bearing right off main road by railway station. This leads down to Vale of Ffestiniog. At Tyn y Cefn you can turn left and then left again to road to Ffestiniog, or you can continue by path down valley to Pont Taly y bont, where you turn left, and a mile on is FFESTINIOG.

Distance 15 miles.

SIXTH DAY

In the neighbourhood of Ffestiniog are many waterfalls, well worth seeing: Cynfal Falls, Rhaiadr Cwm Fall, Raven Fall, and the Roman camp at Tomen y Mur, and Llyn y Morynion—" Lake of the Maidens "—with its legend akin to that of the Sabine women. To reach Beddgelert go along Portmadoc road ½ mile. Where it turns sharp right a path leads past the monument to Pont Tal y bont. Cross over main road and lane leads over river to Tan y Bwlch Hotel. Blocking flank of valley to north is Moelwyn (2,527 ft.). Road continues round Llyn Mair. Just past railway station an old road cuts across the flanks of Moelwyn Bach and past Ogof Llechwin. Road crosses a shoulder of Moelwyn and passes chapel at Tre-saethon in Cwm Croesor, climbs again across a shoulder of Cynicht, the peak north of Moelwyn. From Bwlch-gwernog the old bridle way continues to Bryntirion through sylvan scenery and then emerges on main Beddgelert-Portmadoc road, ¼ mile south of Pont Aberglaslyn. Here, at the famous pass, sheer rocky cliffs, dotted with fir-trees, rise hundreds of feet above the river on either side. From bridge walk along east side of stream to BEDDGELERT— " The Grave of Gelert ". Its Welsh name recalls the story of Llewelyn and his dog, and some stones mark the grave of this faithful animal.

Distance 15 miles.

SEVENTH DAY

To avoid the main road to Llyn Gwynant walk back to Pont Aberglaslyn, and follow bridle-way to Bwlch-gwernog. Here turn left along old pony track up Nantmor Valley, with the high range of Cynicht on right. After 3 miles track turns left at Afon Llyn-eddno; cross stream, and continue along path through woods to main road by Llyn Gwynant. Beyond the lake rise the Snowdon summits, and the celebrated Watkin Path leads up Cwm y Llan almost directly opposite. (Note for those wishing to climb the highest mountain in Wales; there are at least twenty routes, as well as a mountain railway. Snowdon is not a single summit, for the mountain so-called has three peaks all over 3,000 feet. Highest point is Y Wyddfa (3,560 ft.). The other two are Garnedd Ugain (3,493 ft.) and Crib Goch (3,023 ft.). A popular route is the Pyg Track which starts opposite hotel at Pen y Pas, 4 miles farther on.

Direct route from Llanberis is the easiest route. For a good description of view from summits read George Borrow's *Wild Wales*. To continue our itinerary: from foot of Lake Gwynant leave main road and follow old road skirting the Afon Glaslyn. After 2 miles, and just before rejoining main road again, track will be seen bearing left over stream to main Llanberis—Capel Curig road at Pen-y-Pas (hotel). Turn left for Llanberis. Two miles on is Old Llanberis. LLANBERIS (modern) lies a mile farther on. From Llanberis to Caernarvon is 9 miles (by bus).

Distance 15 miles.

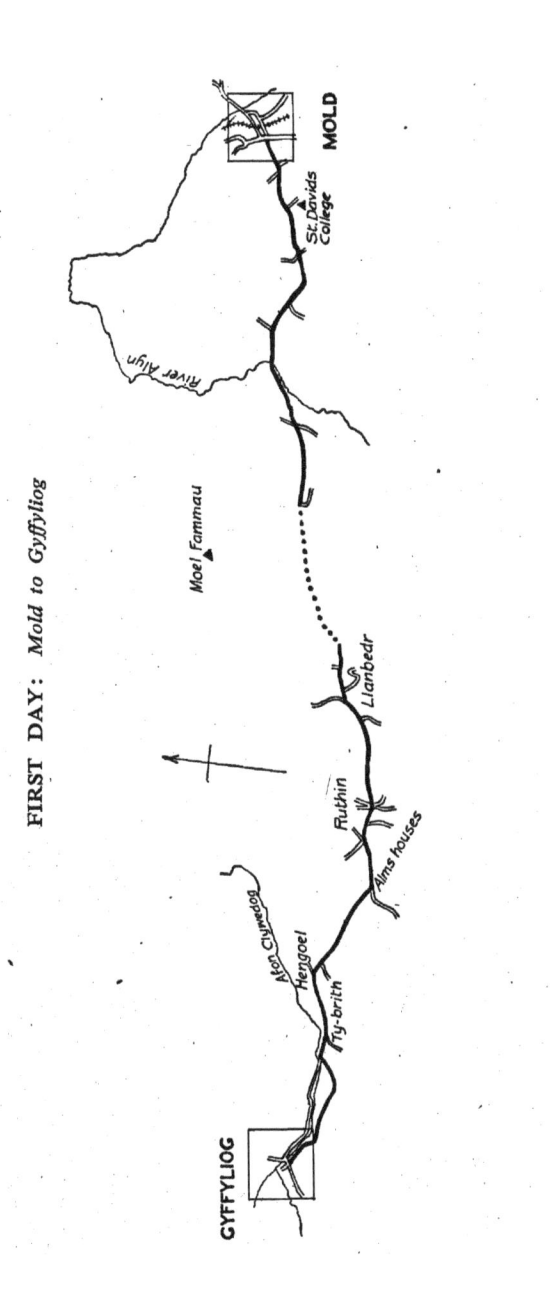

FIRST DAY: *Mold to Gyffyliog*

SECOND DAY: Gyffyliog to Llansanna

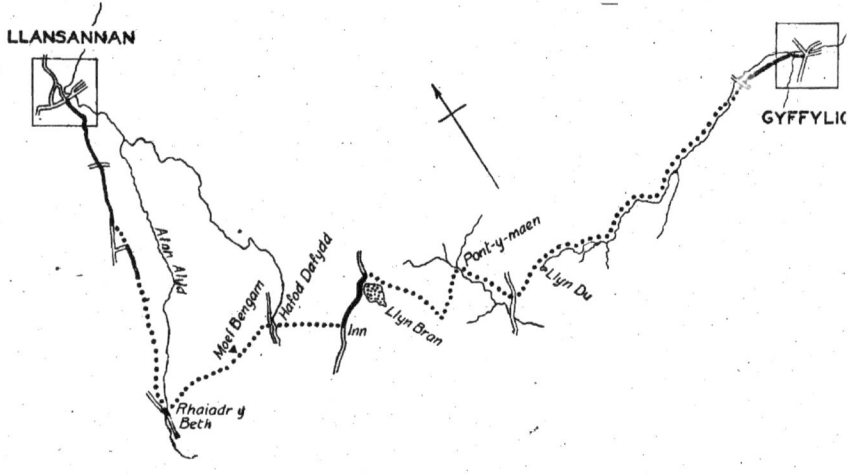

THIRD DAY: Llansannan to Llanrwst

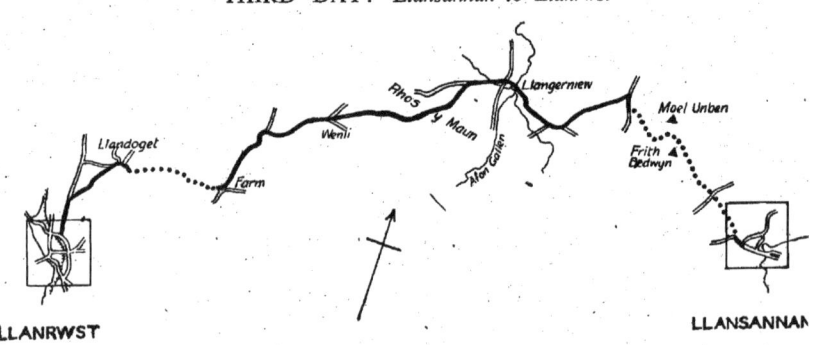

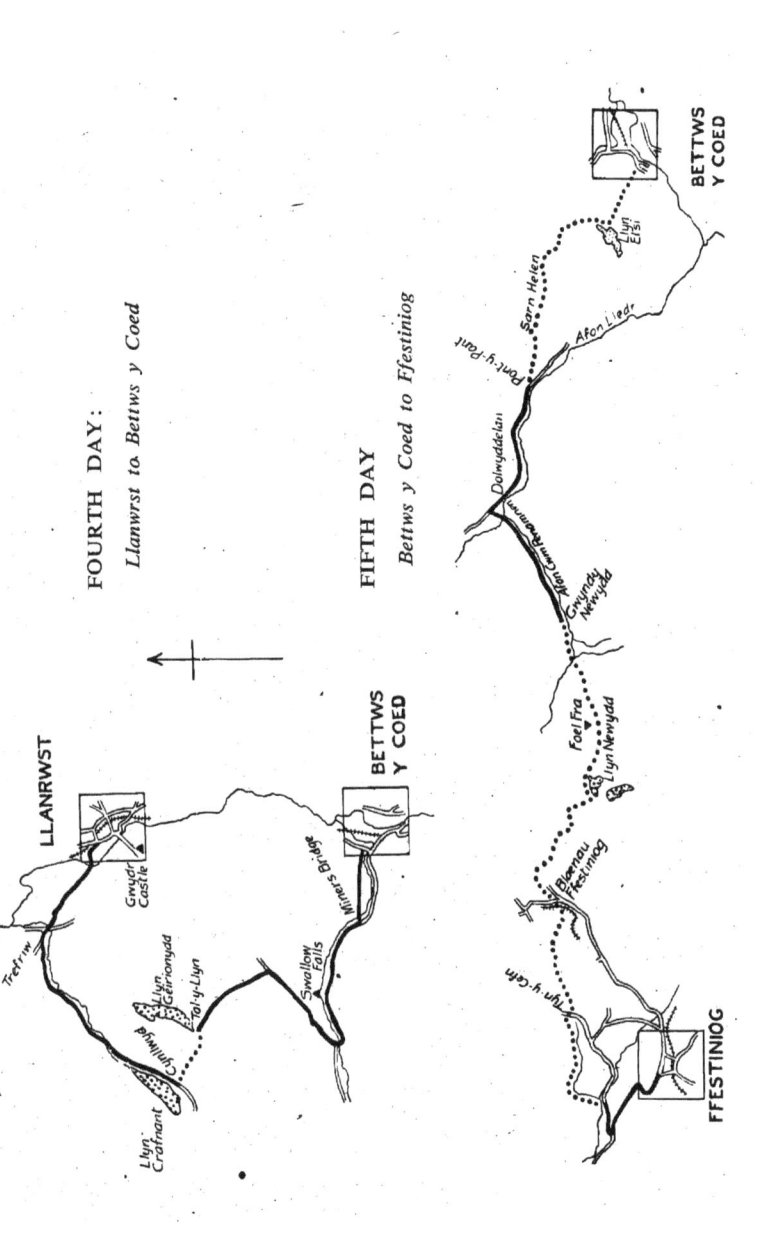

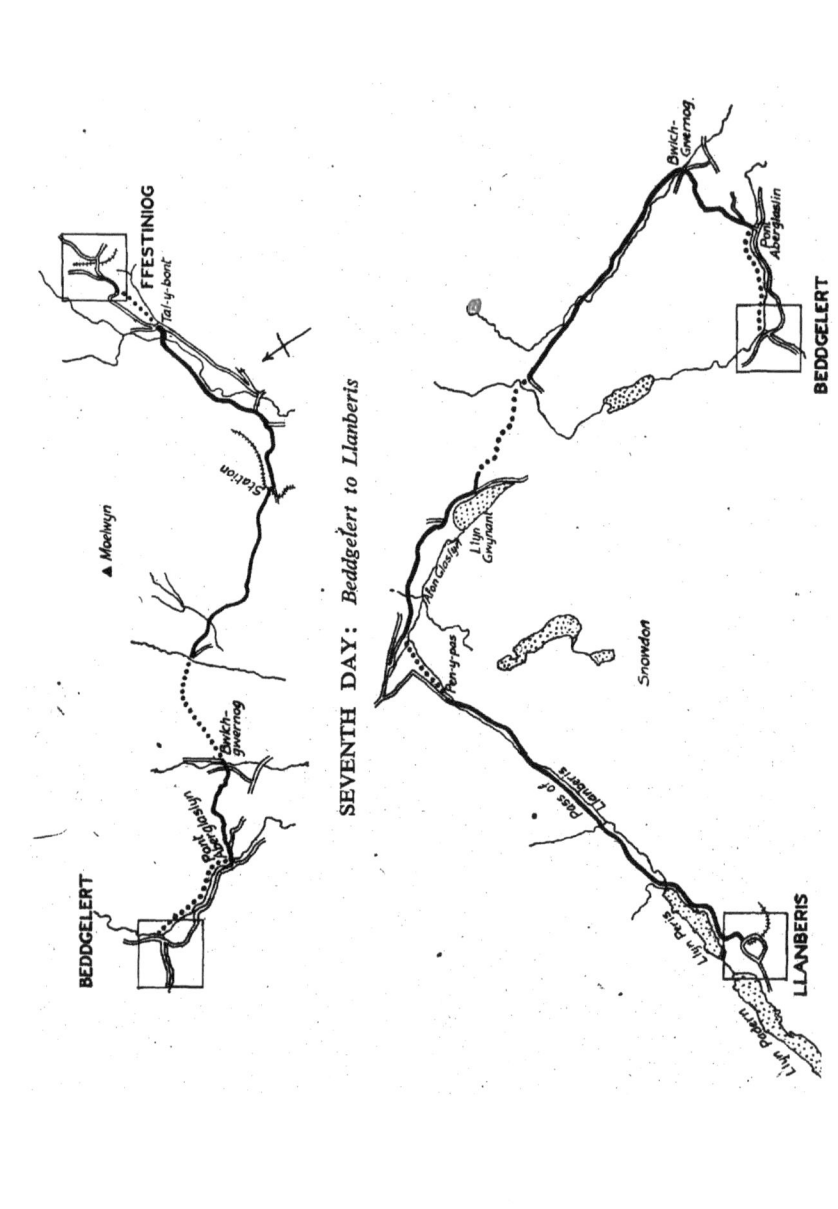

SEVENTH DAY: *Beddgelert to Llanberis*

4. UNSPOILT DORSET

Dorset is my favourite English county. It is so unspoilt and old-world, and then it has the strong literary interest of being the Hardy country. Having explored almost every corner of Dorset, I detail one tour, and if its charm appeals to you, then there are other equally appealing places for you to visit. One especially intoxicating scene is to see the Dorset heath in bloom, and I can well appreciate why Lawrence of Arabia decided on making his home there—in a corner of England where time itself seems to have stood still.

Summary of distances

1. DORCHESTER TO MORETON STATION . . 9 miles
2. WAREHAM . . . . . . 14 „
3. WIMBORNE . . . . . . 12 „
4. CRANBORNE . . . . . . 14 „
5. BLANDFORD . . . . . . 14 „
6. STURMINSTER NEWTON . . . . 15 „
7. SHERBORNE . . . . . . 14 „

   Total Distance. . . . . 92 „

Train travel

Dorchester. S.R. and G.W.R.
Sherborne. S.R.

Bus travel

Wilts and Dorset Motor Services, Ltd.
Southern National Omnibus Company, Ltd.
Western National Omnibus Company, Ltd.

Maps

One-inch Ordnance Survey sheet 8, 178, 179 (N.P.).

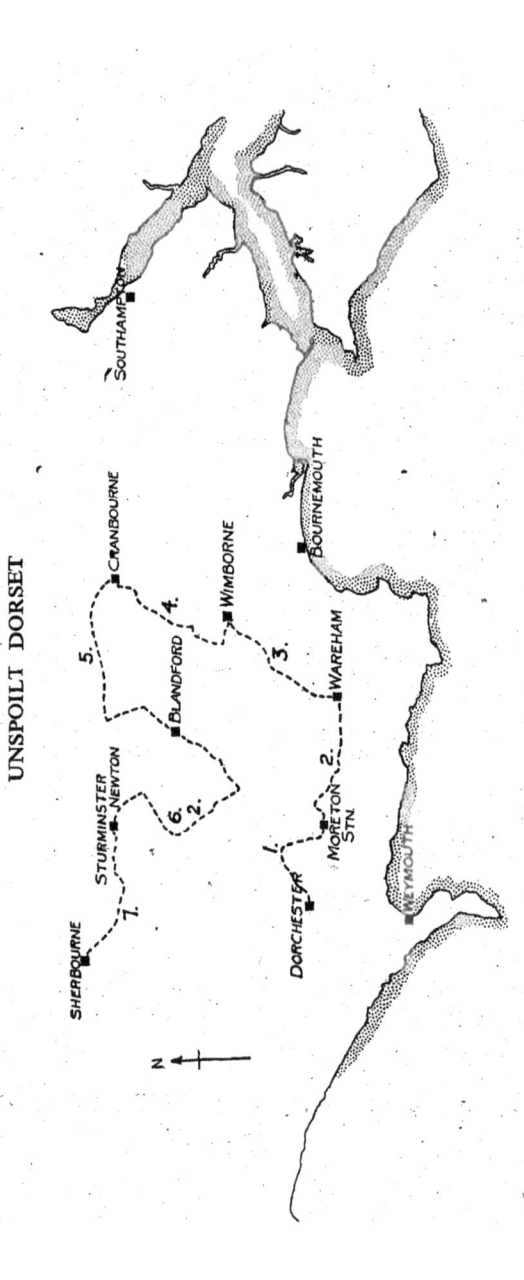

FIRST DAY

Leave Dorchester by the Bere Regis road and just beyond Grey's Bridge, turn right by footpath across three meadows to Stinsford, the Mellstock of Thomas Hardy, and the place where his heart is buried with his first wife. In the south aisle of the tiny church is a memorial window to the writer. Continue by the stream and cross it into Lower Bockhampton, continuing northwards over the cross-roads to the junction up the hill, where turn right through Higher Bockhampton. At the end of the village, shyly hiding itself under heavy thatch, is the cottage where Hardy was born. Follow the path beyond, up to the ridge half-way alongside Yellowham Wood, where turn right to Puddletown, thus avoiding the main road. Descending White Hill towards the village, keep right, join the main road to right—leaving the village on left—and almost immediately bear right. (The road to left leads to Tolpuddle, the home of the agricultural "martyrs" of 1834). One mile on, bear right for Tincleton, beyond which cross the River Frome, take first left, and ½ mile beyond, bear right for MORETON STATION (and the "Frampton Arms").

Distance 9 miles.

SECOND DAY

Turn in a north-easterly direction and take first turn on right for Moreton. Turn right in the village and a few yards further on, on the right, is a small plot of ground containing a few graves. At the far end of this, on the right, is the resting-place of Lawrence of Arabia. To reach Clouds Hill, the cottage he occupied for a time before his death—which is open to the public—go back to the village and enquire the way across the river, then ascend through the rhododendrons. At the far end when a road is encountered, turn right, then right at next turning—the cottage being immediately on left. Continue on this road, descending through Bovington to the River Frome.

Before crossing the grand old stone bridge, note Tess's farmhouse—the old home of the real d'Urberville family. Beyond the railway turn left, but do not enter Wool, continuing instead by Holme Lane that passes the entrance to Bindon Abbey—the remains of a twelfth century Cistercian house. Beyond, traverse Stoke Common, leave West Holme and East Holme on your left, and at the far end of a wood, turn left and so gain WAREHAM, enclosed within its ancient earth-walls.
Distance 14 miles.

THIRD DAY

Leave by the bridge over the River Piddle, north of the town, and, beyond the station, bear right and at next fork, bear left by the pottery works. By the side of these, a footpath goes off to the right, across Gore Heath. At $1\frac{1}{4}$ miles by a pond the way forks; take that to the right and make for Organ Ford, keeping left. At $\frac{1}{2}$ mile on, gain the main road, cross it diagonally to the left and continue northward for Lytchett Matravers, a scattered village that lies mostly to the west. Keep right for Barrow Hill and so through Stony Down Plantation. Drop down beyond it, pass over cross-roads, cross stream and accompany it for $\frac{1}{4}$ mile, then climb steeply to the left, to pass over the main road by the violet farm. The road passes Merley Hall on left, and at next cross-roads, by tiny post office, turn left for WIMBORNE MINSTER, the history of which goes back to Saxon days. The minster is famous for its chained library and the astronomical clock made in 1320.
Distance 12 miles.

FOURTH DAY

On leaving the town in a north-westerly direction, note the quaint little chapel of St. Margaret's Hospital adjoining the almshouses. Keep right of this and mount by a road that skirts Kingston Lucy Park, and then becomes a tunnel under beech trees. A short way ahead, an opening to the right gives

UNSPOILT DORSET

access to Badbury Rings, an encampment of triple ramparts, from the topmost of which extensive views are obtained. It was here that King Arthur, so legend says, defeated the Saxons in A.D. 520. North-easterly lies Witchampton, to reach which, go forward by the ancient trackway that runs straight as a die towards Old Sarum. From the picturesque village on the bank of the River Allen, skirt Crichel Park, glimpsing the house by its large lake, when on its north side. Beyond, at the road junction, turn right, then left, pass a farm, and by the stream, turn right by a track that leads to another farm, beyond which after turning left for a few yards along the lane, a footpath continues in the main direction to Wimborne St. Giles, lying at the park gates of the home of Lord Shaftesbury—a house dating from 1561. Beyond the village, take the second turning on the right and so reach CRANBORNE.
Distance 14 miles.

FIFTH DAY

At the northern end of Cranborne, take the left-hand fork and climb to the top of Pentridge Hill, standing sentinel over the way into the county from Hampshire and Wiltshire, and commanding extensive views over Cranborne Chase. At its foot nestles the village, from which go south, downhill, and follow the track to the right. Almost immediately it divides; here keep right again, uphill. About $\frac{1}{4}$ mile on, an ancient sunken trackway goes to the left in a south-westerly direction; follow this to the road, along which turn right. Where it crosses the main Salisbury—Blandford road at Handley Hill, look for a bus time-table notice board to ascertain when a bus leaves Farnham cross-roads ($3\frac{1}{4}$ miles south-west) for Blandford. Before catching a bus to find a night's lodging, some nine miles have to be walked and much of interest to be seen between Handley Hill and Farnham Cross. Proceed across main road to Handley, the Sixpenny Handley of some old sign-posts. Beyond church, turn right and climb to Woodcutts Common, a tract of heathland, on the edge of Cranborne Chase, and remarkable for remains of Roman-British village, excavated by the late General Pitt-Rivers, whose home was in the nearby Rushmore Park. The road leads over the border into Wiltshire and Tollard Royal, where King John had a hunting lodge. South of the village are Larmer Pleasure Grounds, laid out for the public by General Pitt-Rivers, whilst further south still, on the outskirts of Farnham, is the museum in which he housed his archaeological finds and scale models of excavated sites. (Admission fee.) Continue southwards until the road crosses the main road, where await the bus that will take you to the right to BLANDFORD and to bed.

Distance 14 miles.

SIXTH DAY

As this will be a long day, take an early bus to Winterborne Whitchurch, where keep right of the church and ascend gradually for 2¼ miles; then turn left and descend through the tree-embowered Milton Abbas, a 200-years-old example that might well be copied by those responsible for replanning and rehousing our present-day communities. This is a simple but stately village, replacing a small market town that clustered too closely round the home of the first Earl of Dorchester. He allowed the Abbey church to stand and on certain days of the week entrance may be obtained to it and the delightful park in which it stands. To the north-west lies Hilton and beyond Ansty Cross. At the first road junction, turn right and ascend Bulbarrow Hill—with an unlimited view all round from its height of 902 feet. Turn right and north-eastward to walk along the ridge as far as Okeford Hill, then descend into Okeford Fitzpaine. In this village of thatched brickwork, turn left, then right, and so through Broad Oak and steeply down to the twin places of STURMINSTER NEWTON, separated by the River Stour, but joined by a long bridge. It was in the rambling town north of the river, that William Barnes went to school and, later, worked for a solicitor.

Distance 15 miles.

SEVENTH DAY

Westward, between the Stour and the Lydden, lies Bagber Common, where Barnes spent his childhood; but from Newton, take the road southward and ½ mile on, at River Corner, turn left and follow the road uphill to the fork at the top, where keep right, descend to cross the River Divelish by its old bridge, near which a Roman pavement was discovered some years ago. Beyond is Fifehead Neville, where Grace Scott, Barnes' mother, was born. At next road junction, turn left and ½ mile on, bear right for Kingston. Turn right, go downhill across a stream, then turn right through Woodrow to King's Stag Bridge, where, according to tradition, King Henry III spared the life of a white hart. Subsequently the bailiff of the forest killed it and incurred the King's wrath. He was imprisoned and the district was fined in perpetuity—a tax that became known as White Hart Silver. Beyond, pass over the cross-roads and so come to Crouch Hill, where turn right. At Barnes Cross, go right and keep left beyond the Caundle Brook. At next cross-roads, turn left to Bishop's Down. Take second turn on right and instead of going right again down to Kitford Bridge, keep straight on over a lane and a few yards ahead, bear right by a footpath that leads to Folke. Turn left, then right and go forward to SHERBORNE—one-time capital of Wessex, now a pleasant market town, clustering round its ancient Abbey and School.

Distance 14 miles.

FIRST DAY: *Dorchester to Moreton*

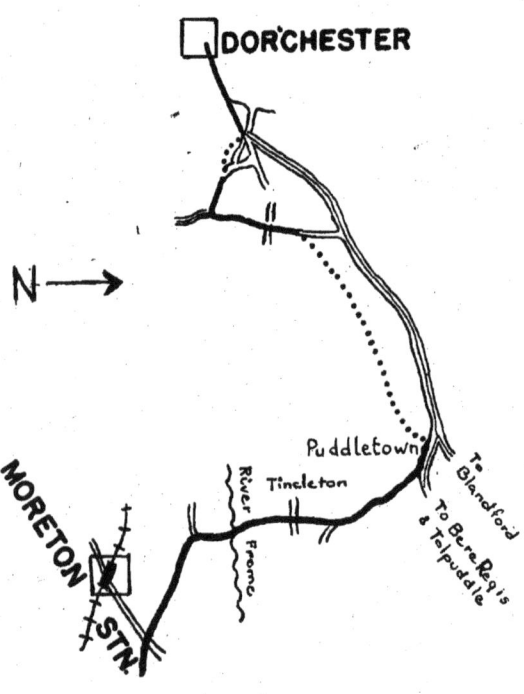

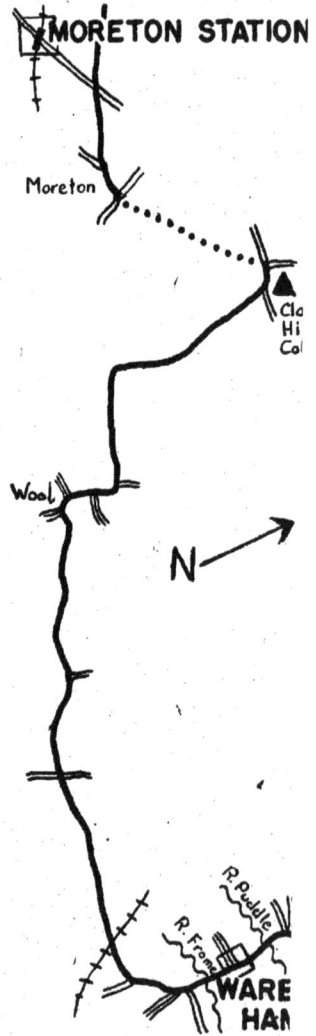

SECOND DAY: *Moreton to Wareham*

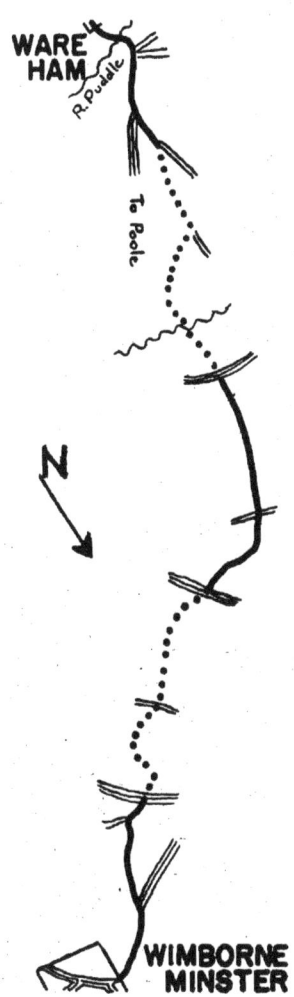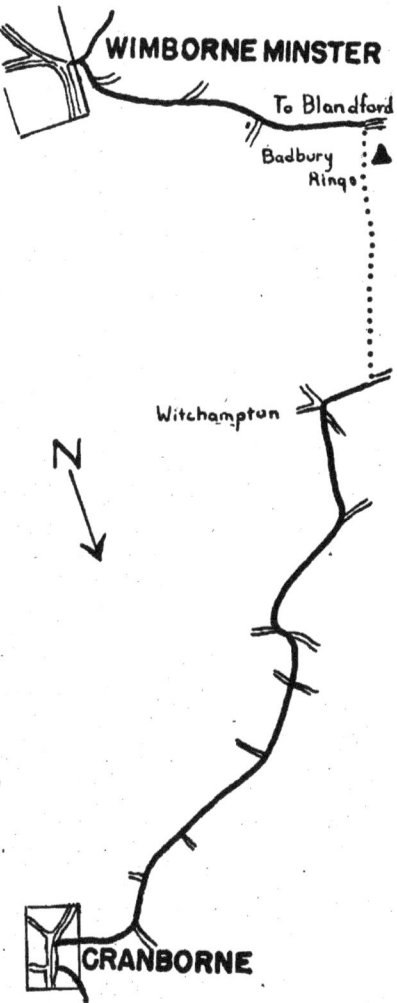

THIRD DAY:
Wareham to Wimborne Minster

FOURTH DAY:
Wimborne Minster to Cranborne

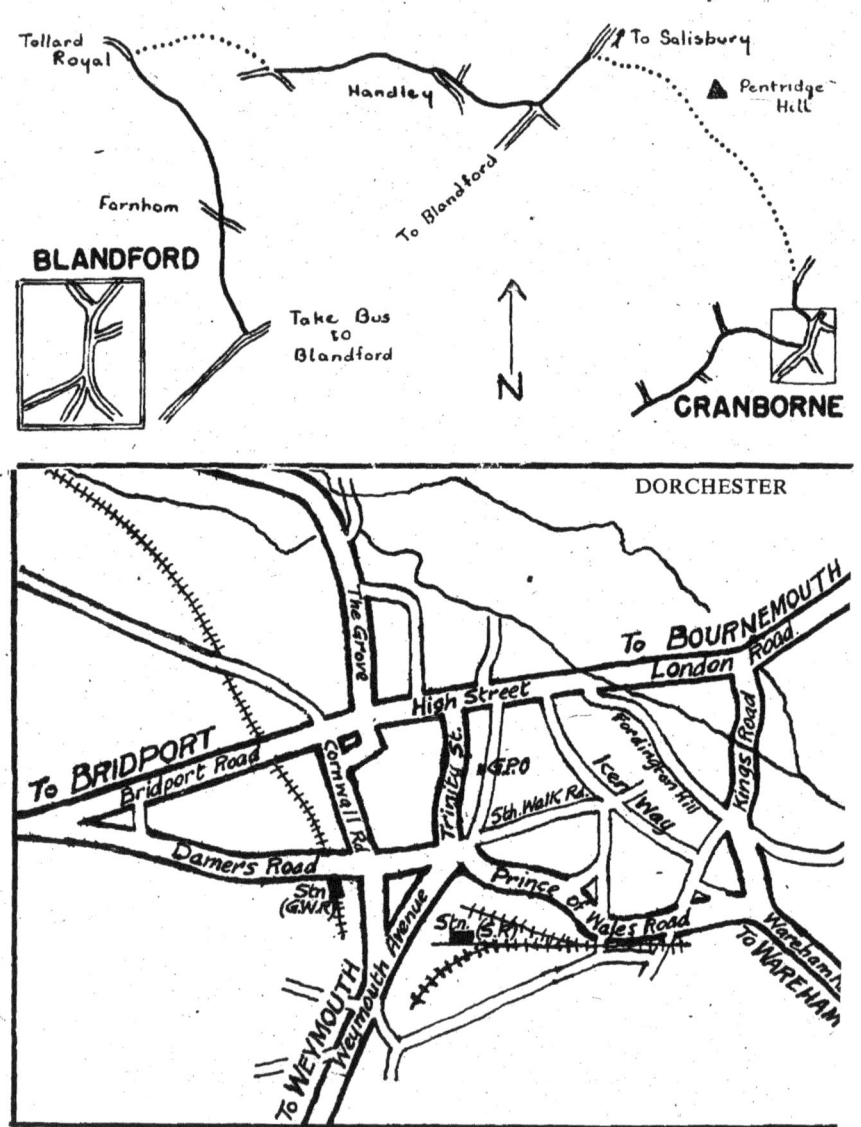

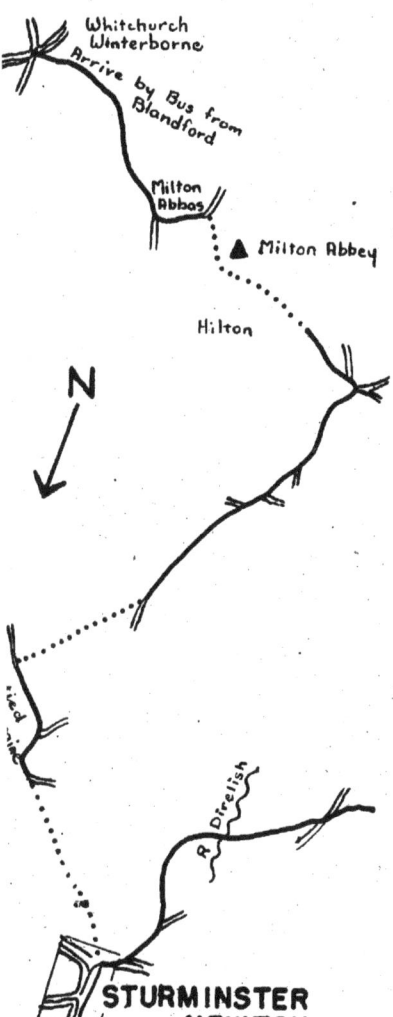
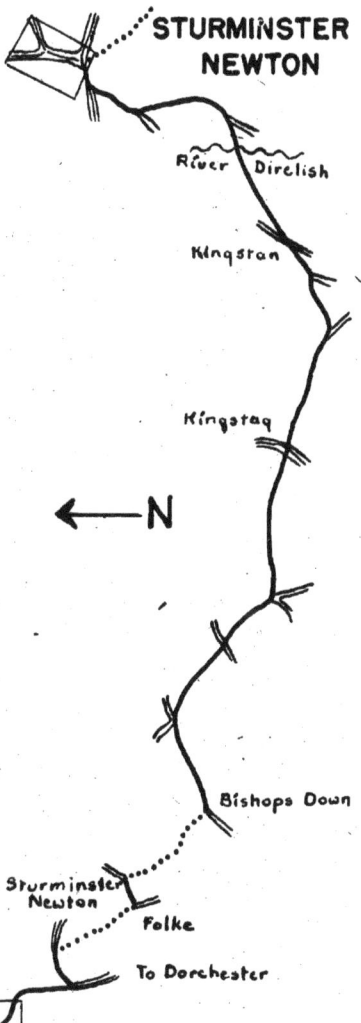

5. THE WYE VALLEY

As the Wye Valley is largely the borderland between England and Wales, it has naturally been the scene of stirring events from the earliest times; so that, in addition to its natural beauty, which is world-famous, it is also extremely rich in historical interest. There is a wide variety for the hiker on this tour, including a considerable detour through the Forest of Dean, which still retains some of the atmosphere of the old English woodland.

Summary of distances

1. CHEPSTOW TO MONMOUTH . . . . 16 miles
2. One-day tour via King's Wood, Dingestow, Craig-Y-Dorth and Penallt, returning to MONMOUTH . . . . . . 12 „
3. Three-day tour through the Forest of Dean to BLAKENEY, and via . . . . 14 „
4. Cockshoot Wood to MITCHELDEAN and via 14 „
5. Nailbridge back to MONMOUTH . . 15 „
6. Ross . . . . 15 „
7. HEREFORD . . . . . . 15 „

Total Distance 101

Train travel
Chepstow and Hereford. G.W.R.

Bus travel
Red and White Services, Ltd.
Bristol/ Tramways.

MAPS
One-inch Ordnance Survey, sheets 91, 92, 102, 103.

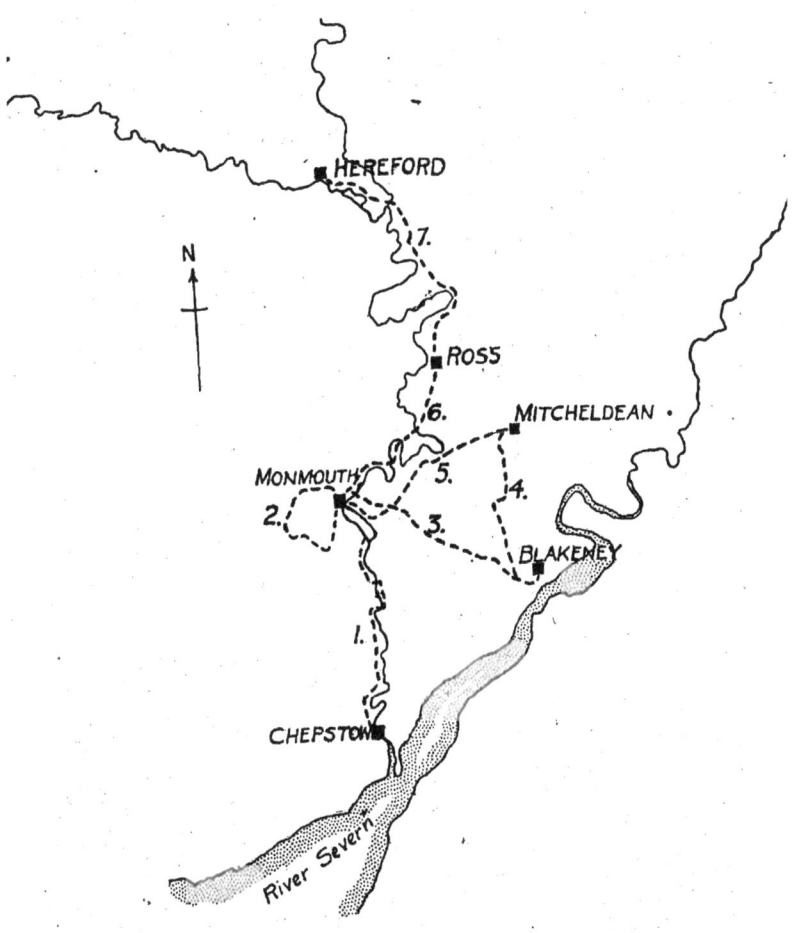

FIRST DAY

Chepstow is a fascinating old town, the great object of interest being the ancient castle. Leave the town by the main Monmouth road, passing the interesting old Town Gate. A mile farther on, at a roundabout, turn right, and, passing the racecourse, continue towards St. Arvan's (hotel). Turn right before reaching the church, and continue for ¼ mile. Ignore the right turn here, and take the forward road until you reach a junction of the ways. Now go forward again by a winding main track, which leads you on to the Wynd Cliff, a natural platform on the summit of a hill, 800 feet above the level of the River Wye below. Before you is a breath-taking prospect, a wonderful landscape which is one of the most beautiful in England. On leaving, return again to the junction of the ways, and now turn right along a path which leads you to Porth-gaseg Farm. Turn left down a road here for ¼ mile until you pass a pond on your left. Now turn right along a track which in 1½ miles brings you to Tintern Abbey. This world-famous abbey, founded in 1131 by the Cistercian monks, has a setting which has magic, wonder, charm. In apple-blossom time and under a summer's full moon it has a beauty which is indescribable. If you wish to make Monmouth the same night, you cannot dally in this perfect spot, but must carry on past Tintern Parva, along the main road, until you come to Brockweir Bridge (scene in 1913 of a record for net fishing in the River Wye, when a seventy-year-old fisherman caught 115 salmon in 17 hours). Cross the bridge (inn) and turn immediately left beyond it and follow the path by the Wye for over 3 miles until you arrive at Bigsweir Bridge. Cross the Wye again and turn right for ¼ mile. A climbing path on the left now leads you upwards to Whitebrook (inn). From here descend to the river and follow the footpath along the Wye to Penallt Halt (inn). Two-and-a-half miles farther on by the river path is your destination for the night, Monmouth. But, for a change and some fine views, a route over the hill via Penallt Church is recommended. Branch off by a path the near side of the

THE WYE VALLEY

church and you are now rewarded with a wonderful prospect over the Monmouth Vale to the Black Mountains and the various hills beyond. At Troy House you strike the road which brings you to Troy Station and forward to MONMOUTH—a historic town of considerable interest.

(Do not miss visiting the museum with the finest collection of Nelson relics to be seen in the world.)

Distance 16 miles.

SECOND DAY

Crossing the picturesque Monnow Bridge, turn right and walk on for nearly ½ mile. Take a left road opposite a letter-box and, bearing right, continue for about a mile until you reach a lane on the right. Alongside this lane, which has become a watercourse, take a parallel path to its left, crossing the deep lane ½ mile farther on. Now follow the left hedge until you reach Bailey Pit Farm. Beyond it join the track again, taking the right branch which brings you through King's Wood. You now have a mile descent to Tre-Owen, a large Tudor manor-house. Continue your descent to Dingestow Church, and at the cross-roads bear south ¼ mile for the railway station. A ¼ mile beyond turn left on the main road, when in just over a further ¼ mile an inn is reached—the last port of call until Monmouth is reached, 7 miles distant. From the inn carry along the main road for ½ mile, then take the right track from the white gate of Redhouse Farm. Pass this farm, and then take the path diagonally up the field to Trealy Farm. In view of a confusion of paths it is best to ask at this farm the way on to Craig-y-dorth. You now get a magnificent panorama of the countryside below, with the Black Mountains in the distance. Carry on cross-country for ¾ mile until you strike a road which in a mile passes the entrance to the side-road to Lydart House. Half a mile farther on, where the road turns sharp left, take a forward path, which, descending, brings you in due course to the road leading to Troy Station and MONMOUTH.

Distance 12 miles.

THIRD DAY*

During the next three days you have a complete change of scene, for you will walk through the solemn stillness of the woodlands of the Forest of Dean. The demands of two wars have seen much matured timber cut and new plantations taking their place. Here and there you touch on coalmining activities. But there are hours when you will be alone in woodland paths and tracks—where in the Middle Ages robbers found a safe refuge. The commander of the Spanish had orders " not to leave a tree standing in it, if," says John Evelyn, " they should not be able to subdue our nation ". The oaks were particularly valuable for shipbuilding at that time.

Cross the Wye near May Hill Station, take the second road on the left, signposted to Gloucester. Three hundred yards on you strike a footpath, signposted "To the Kymin", ascending through a wood and leading to a road, where take the right branch. At the next bend take the right fork of two forward paths which brings you to the Kymin. This hill is 800 feet high and commands a fine view. It belongs to the National Trust. See the Naval Temple, with medallions of Nelson's admirals, and then proceed on to the Buckstone, near Staunton (hotel). It is the most celebrated rocking-stone in the kingdom. From Staunton proceed for 2 miles south-east through Marian's Inclosure to Colebrooke. From this village a mile on you arrive at Coalway Lane End. Follow right through into the Forest of Dean. The road ends on its edge, but a path takes you for 2 miles to Parkend (inn). A road now takes you through Oakenhill Wood and Cockshoot Wood to Yorkley Slade (inn) and along Viney Hill to Viney. A ¼ mile farther on turn left for Nibley and BLAKENEY.

* For those hikers who prefer an alternative to three days walking through forest I would suggest one day a forest walk (Monmouth–Staunton–Speech House–Coleford–St. Briavels–Llandogo–bus to Monmouth); on the second day Monmouth–Trelleck–Llandogo–bus to Monmouth; and on the third day bus to Abergavenny and Llanvihangel. Then, on foot, by

THE WYE VALLEY 71

Fforest—Garn Wen, Llantony Abbey, Hatteral Hill, Pandy, and return to Llanvihangel.

Distance 14 miles.

FOURTH DAY

From Blakeney retrace yesterday's steps to Viney Hill. Half-way on the road to Yorkley Slade branch off to the right by a path, leading in a north-westerly direction through Cockshoot Wood. Two miles farther on after crossing a railway-line you strike a road again. Turn left at a junction, and after ¼ mile turn right. Two miles on you arrive at the Speech House Hotel. The " Speech House " lies amid miles of beautiful and varied woodlands. It was built in the reign of Charles II for the use of the ancient court of " The Speech ". The Verderers were originally appointed by King Canute, and their court is still held at the " Speech House ", which is now an hotel.

Turn right at the hotel and ½ mile on, at a milestone, bear left on a track, which goes north-easterly to Crabtree Hill. Continue north for over 1½ miles, past Drybrook Road Station until you reach the main Gloucester road. Turn right to Nailbridge, then left, and ½ mile on take the right-hand road to Drybrook. Turn right again, and follow the road to MITCHELDEAN.

Distance 14 miles.

FIFTH DAY

Retrace your steps for ¼ mile, then turn off right for Puddlebrook, distinguishing it from Drybrook nearby. A curious-looking building near Puddlebrook has the equally strange name of " Euroclydon ". A road and path now brings you in 2 miles to Ruardean (inn). Ruardean Hill reaches a height of 932 feet, the highest in the Forest of Dean, and from here you get a most magnificent panorama in all directions. From Ruardean descend by road and path to Lower Lydbrook (inn), continue on to English Bicknor, and then on to the

Coleford road for a mile, bearing right then to Short Standing (inn). By path and track you can now walk over Coalpit Hill to Staunton, just over a mile distant. At Staunton walk south. At fork, ½ mile on, bear right, and after passing under railway bridge join road, turn right, and at Redbrook Station right again. Now follow the road along the Wye to Wyesham and back to MONMOUTH.

Distance 15 miles.

SIXTH DAY

From Monmouth follow the river-path along the Wye on its north bank, past King Arthur's Cave, Seven Sisters Rocks and Lord's Wood to Symonds Yat—a distance of about 6 miles. Crossing is by ferry. The panorama from the Yat Rock is famous, although the environment suffers by reason of the litter scattered around by visitors! Here the Wye makes a big loop, and it is only about 600 yards to the other side of it. There is a river footpath. Walk north up the loop for 1¼ miles. Cross at the road-bridge to Goodrich (inn). (Alternatively you can follow river-path from Symonds Yat to Welsh Bicknor, and there cross the Wye for Goodrich.) From Goodrich (Kerne Bridge) I will offer two more alternate ways of reaching Ross. Either you follow the road to Glewstone (2 miles) and then follow the river-path which takes you to Ross; or you cross the Kerne Bridge, turn left for ½ mile (before you reach an inn), then by footpath to Coughton. From here follow the left outside edge of Chase Wood for just over a mile until you strike a road leading left. This brings you on to the main road, and ½ mile afterwards into ROSS.

Distance 15 miles.

SEVENTH DAY

The Wye Valley between Ross and Hereford is less spectacular than between Chepstow and Ross, but it is still very

THE WYE VALLEY 73

beautiful. If preferred, hikers could start their tour at Hereford, and then build up to the climax of Tintern.

Ross itself is an ancient place, with some interesting old buildings and customs. Leave the town by a road which runs due north to Hill of Eaton. The Ordnance Survey map shows paths parallel to the road on the left which can be taken. At Hill of Eaton another path to the right of the road brings you to Hole-in-the-Wall, a small hamlet, and the River Wye. A river footpath or the adjoining road leads on to How Caple (meaning "Hugh's Chapel"). Continue straight on after the cross-roads to Brockhampton and Capler Wood. A mile farther on is Fownhope (inn). Here there is an impressive parish church. A path branching off to the right-hand in the village takes you up to Common Hill ($\frac{1}{4}$ mile), from which there is a fine prospect. Proceed north $\frac{1}{2}$ mile until you reach a road; then turn left and right again on a path which you meet just before coming to a big wood. This path runs up to Littlehope between two big woods. At Littlehope continue to Mordiford, where you cross the River Wye. Hereford is 3 miles distant. About half-way from Mordiford you strike a river-bank footpath on the left, and it brings you almost to Hereford.

HEREFORD has an interesting cathedral and some other ancient buildings. Local guides give descriptive details.

Distance 15 miles.

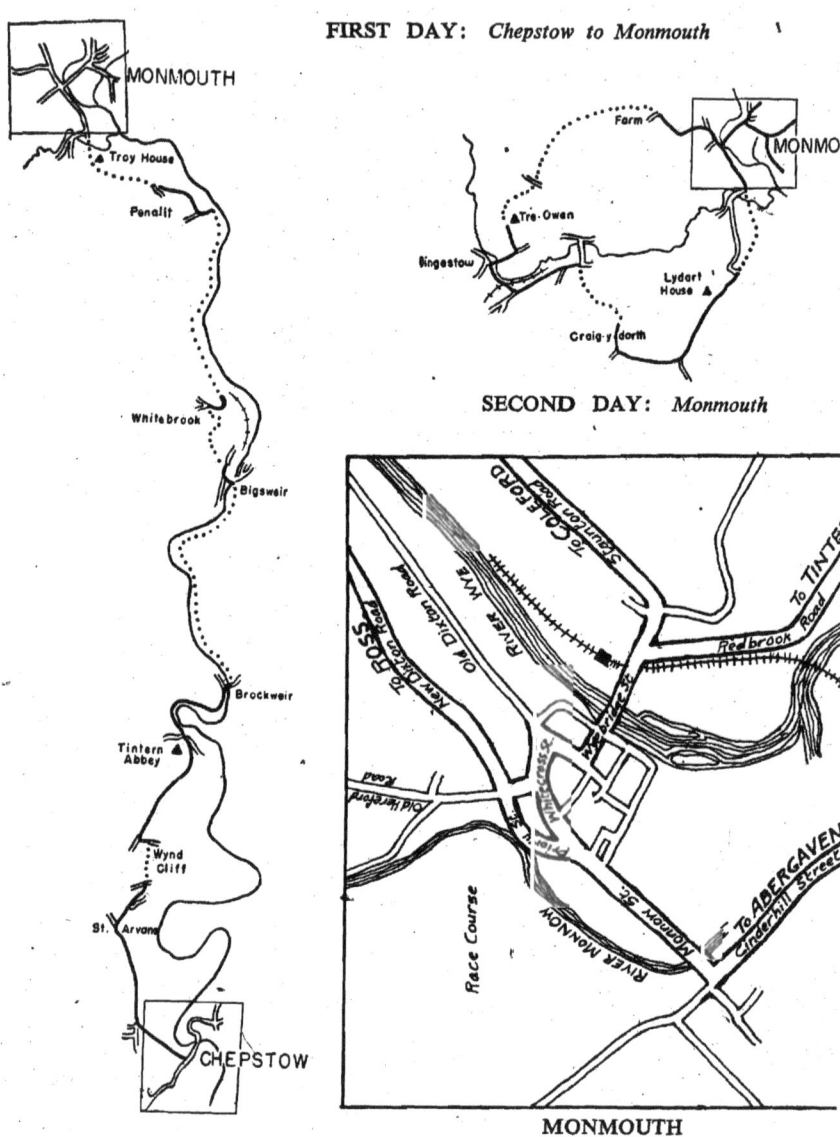

FIRST DAY: *Chepstow to Monmouth*

SECOND DAY: *Monmouth*

THIRD DAY: *Monmouth to Blakeney*

FOURTH DAY: *Blakeney to Mitcheldean*

FIFTH DAY: *Mitcheldean to Monmouth*

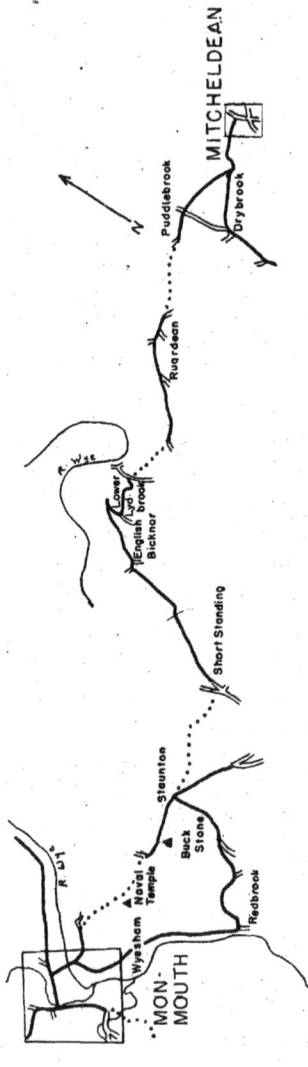

SIXTH DAY: *Monmouth to Ross*

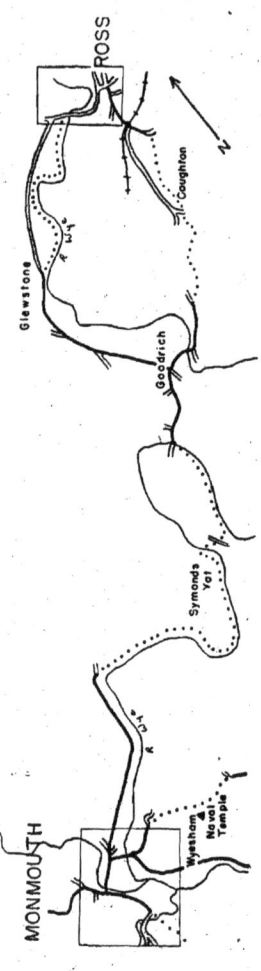

SEVENTH DAY: *Ross to Hereford*

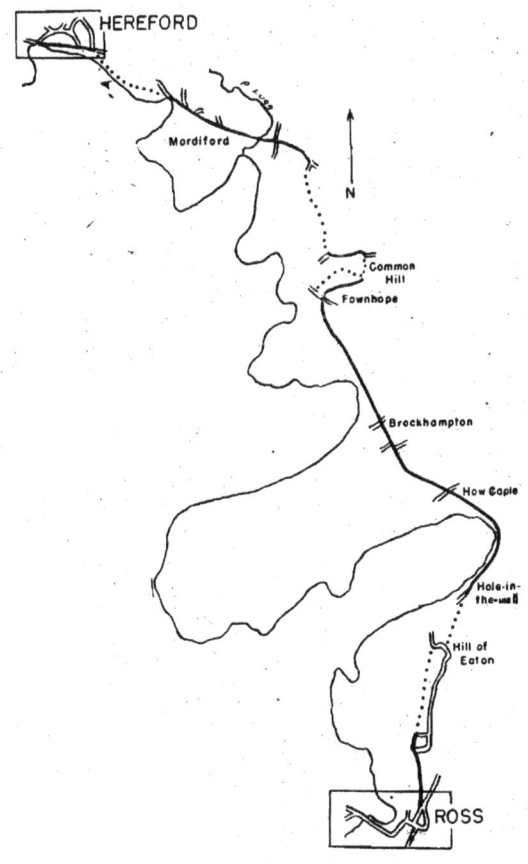

6. "THE LITTLE ENGLAND BEYOND WALES"—THE PEMBROKESHIRE COAST

Little-known, remote, and consequently unspoilt, the Pembrokeshire coast offers the more adventurous hiker a peculiar sense of freedom from our civilization. For here is to be found some of the finest sea-cliff scenery in England, surrounded by an atmosphere of loneliness.

Just because it is rather " out of the world " accommodation is not so easily found as in more tourist areas, but this can be overcome by resourcefulness, and, in fact, to those who think like me, may well prove to be an attraction—for it is an escape from the crowd. Actually the designation "Little England Beyond Wales" only applies to that part of Pembrokeshire south of Solva. It was in this area that Henry I evacuated completely the Welsh population, replacing them with English and Flemish settlers. The Welsh language is not spoken in this district.

Summary of distances
1. TENBY TO MANORBIER . . . . 10 miles
2. MILFORD HAVEN . . . . . 11 ,,
3. LITTLE HAVEN . . . . . 15 ,,
4. ST. DAVID'S . . . . . . 15 ,,
5. TREVINE (TREFAIN) . . . . 14 ,,
6. FISHGUARD . . . . . . 15 ,,.
7. NEWPORT (or CARDIGAN) . . . 14 ,,

      Total Distance   94 ,,

Train travel
Tenby and Cardigan. G.W.R.

Bus travel
West Welsh Omnibus Company, Ltd.

Maps
One-inch Ordnance Survey, sheets 88 and 99.

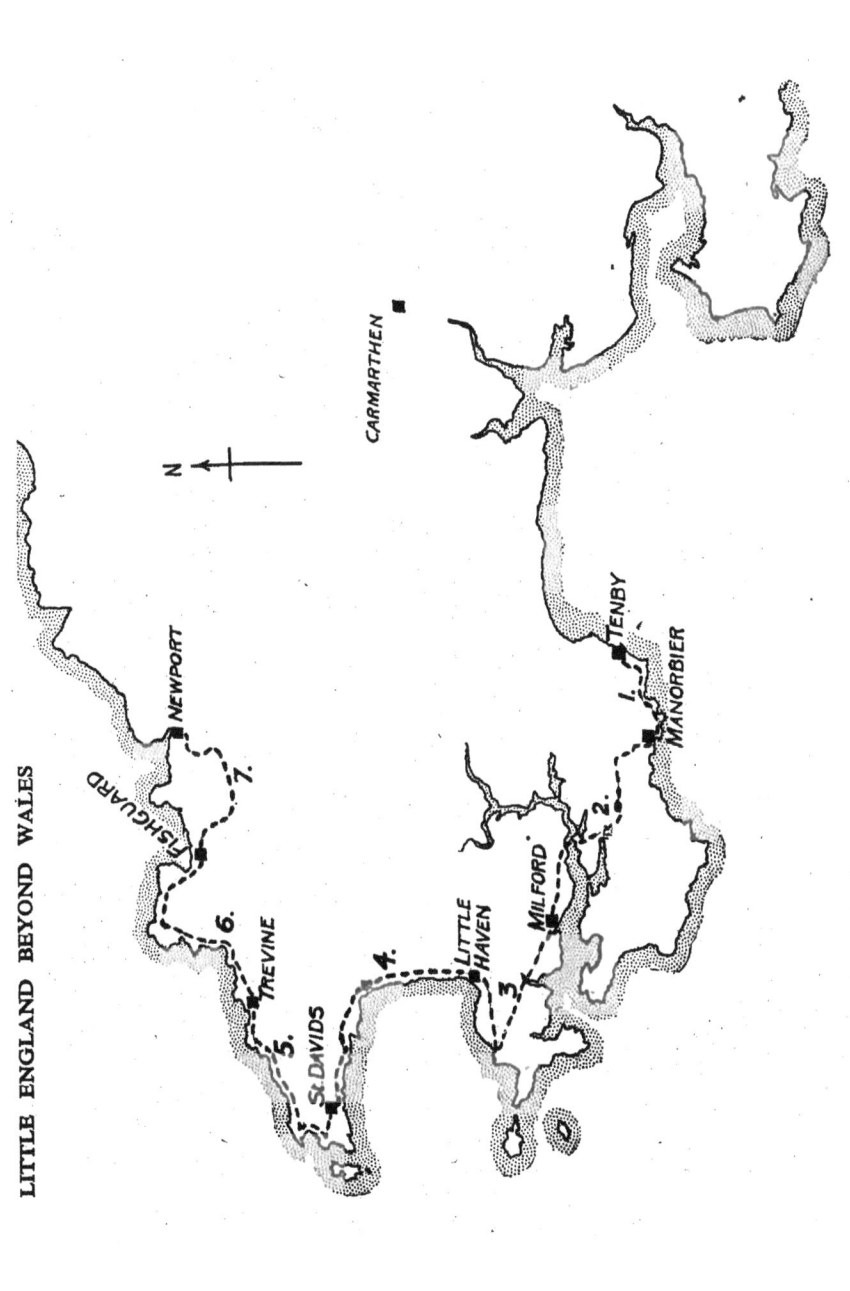

LITTLE ENGLAND BEYOND WALES

FIRST DAY

Though Tenby is a popular holiday resort, it still presents a picturesque appearance with its old walls and gates and fragments of the castle. Excursions can be made to the caves at Hoyle's Mouth and Caldy (island) with its ancient monastery (still occupied by monks).

On leaving Tenby take the path across the golf-course to Penally, with its old church and Celtic cross. Circle round the rifle range to the coast path from Giltar Point which takes you on to the striking headland of Proud Giltar and then to Lydstep Point—the village of Lydstep lying about half a mile away on your right. On the coast here are great caverns carved by the sea in the carboniferous limestone cliffs. The route continues to Skrinkle Haven, Old Castle Head, with its ancient British camp, and the Priest's Nose (more caves). Not far from the Priest's Nose is the very pretty bay at Manorbier Strand. Here you turn up the old road to MANORBIER village, less than ½ mile distant. On the coast note the change from carboniferous limestone to old red sandstone. The contrast between the red rocks and the blue waters on a sunny day is enchanting. At Manorbier there is the castle built by the de Barri family late in the thirteenth century. This was the birthplace of Gerald of Wales.

Distance 10 miles

SECOND DAY*

From Manorbier follow the old road leading north from Manorbier Strand to Jameston (inn), and then follow a road which leads in a north-westerly direction to Manorbier Newton. Just after entering this village turn right along a road which will lead you, by climbing a hill, to Carew Beacon. Returning to the main Tenby-Pembroke main road, walk west for 1¼ miles until you reach the ruins of Lamphey Palace, built by the Bishops of St. David's in the fourteenth century. From here take a footpath which leads you into Lamphey village, ½ mile away. Walk or bus the remaining 2 miles to Pembroke.

"LITTLE ENGLAND BEYOND WALES"

Pembroke Castle is well worth a visit, for it used to be one of the most notable in the country, being known as the "Gibraltar of South Wales". The earliest portion dates from the twelfth century. A short distance out of Pembroke are the ruins of Monkton Priory, which dates from shortly after the Norman Conquest. Take the bus to Pembroke Dock, a naval establishment, and ferry from Hobb's Point to Neyland. From here bus or walk the 4 miles to MILFORD HAVEN, a fishing port of some importance.

* A very fine coastal alternative walk is from Manorbier to St. Govan's Head, and thence to Pembroke.

Distance (walking) 11 miles.

THIRD DAY

Cross Milford Haven harbour by the bridge, and continue along the main road to the village of Hubberston. Half a mile farther on, just after the road takes a sharp right bend north, there is a footpath going west. Follow this for 1 mile to the village of Herbrandston (inn), which overlooks the wide fjord of Milford Haven. Near the inn a road leads to the ferry which takes you across Sandy Haven Pill, then on through Sandy Haven (inn), and from there walk along the coast until halfway across Lindsway Bay there is a footpath which turns north to St. Ishmael's. Route still carries on north to traverse the peninsula from the Haven to St. Bride's. Bride's Bay by way of Mabesgate, Butterhill, and field path from there right through Slatemill Bridge, Pearson Farm, to St. Bride's. St. Bride's is an old monastic settlement with church and old monastic walled garden. From St. Bride's follow path along coastline north along the bay to Broadmoor, where you then take the road for Talbenny. From this village take the road to Falling Cliff and ¾ mile farther on LITTLE HAVEN (inn) is reached.

Distance 15 miles.

FOURTH DAY

Follow the coastal road north for a mile until you reach Sleek Stone, the beginning of a coastguard path, which takes you to Black Point, ½ mile farther on. At Black Point is an ancient *rath* or cliff-top fortress. From here on for the next 5 miles to Newgale (inn) you should have no difficulty, for you simply follow the coast, either by footpath, track, or road. Leaving Newgale follow road or line of cliffs north-west to Points Castle, then the old road to Lochvane, St. Elvis Farm, and on to Solva (inn). Solva village is prettily situated on a sheltered creek. From Solva take the coast footpath again, visiting The Cradle, Porth y Rhaw (old camp), Norfa Common, and Trelerw. This is a picturesque and much indented coast with numerous bays and headlands, many of them crowned by ancient forts, a reminder of the turbulent days most of this countryside saw in the past. At St. Non's Bay is the ruined chapel of St. Non, mother of St. David, and a Holy Well. On the far side of this small bay there is a footpath which leads you to ST. DAVID'S, the smallest cathedral city in Britain (population under 2,000), and lying in a somewhat desolate landscape which is exposed to the full force of the Atlantic gales. There is, however, much of interest to see in this small place including the fine Bishop's Palace.

Distance 15 miles.

FIFTH DAY

This is going to be a strenuous day, unless you can spare an extra day and, with St. David's as your base for a further night, make a more leisurely exploration of the really glorious surrounding coastal scenery. However, on the assumption that you must stick to the itinerary, you will leave St. David's by the road due west which brings you in 2 miles to Porth Stinian, with its lifeboat station and ruined pilgrimage chapel dedicated to St. Justinian. It is also the landing-place for boats to the rocky island of Ramsey, famous for its colonies of sea-birds. From here follow the coast north to Whitesand

"LITTLE ENGLAND BEYOND WALES"

Bay and St. David's Head, the most westerly point in Wales. Here there are considerable prehistoric remains. Climb Carn Llidi (575 ft.) for a grand view of the coast. The country is magnificent with its high cliffs—but the walking is arduous. The whole area contains many prehistoric remains. Follow the coast along for 6 miles to Aber Eiddy, then on to Porthgain. From here the coast runs east for a mile until you strike the main road which leads you into TREVINE (inn).
Distance 14 miles.

SIXTH DAY

From Trevine a mile-long road takes you to Aber-castle. From there take the only road east for ¾ mile until you come to a fork; take the left-hand road which passes over Mynydd Morfa (I hope you may be more successful than I was at speaking these Welsh names!) to Aber Mawr. Follow the coastline north now to Pen Bwch-du and beyond for just over a mile until you strike the road again, which skirts Garn Fawr (678 ft.), with its old camp and view over the lonely countryside, treeless and windswept. Carry on past Treathro until you reach Llanwnwr. Here the road turns right, but you should carry on cross-country to Strumble Head, where there is a lighthouse built on a small island. The cliffs are covered with birds during the nesting season and the area abounds in various rare flowers. Turning east, you follow the coast along for 3 miles to Gwastad Point. Here a pillar marks the spot where the French made a landing on February 22, 1797. This was the last occasion on which a foreign foe landed in Britain. Leaving the coast, you now follow the path to Llanwnda, with its old church and incised stones. Take the old road east from here to Harbour Village and then on ½ mile to Goodwick, the terminus for steamers to Ireland. A mile farther on is FISHGUARD—a journey I personally bussed after the most strenuous walk of the week. Fishguard is often described as a typical old Welsh town. It is certainly a "haven of rest".
Distance 15 miles.

SEVENTH DAY

This last day should find you in the pink of walking condition—for it is again a strenuous one. Leaving Fishguard, you cross the bridge to the Lower Town, and then follow the Newport road for ¾ mile until you strike a lane which turns right to Cilshafe and Llanchyaer Bridge and the wooded Cwm Gwaun valley. This separates the range of the Prescelly Mountains (1,760 ft.) from the coast hills terminating in Mynydd Carn-ingli (1,138 ft.) Cross bridge and proceed ½ mile till you come to cross-roads. Turn left and keep left until you cross Cil-rhndyn bridge. The road then follows the north bank of the stream closely for 4½ miles to Llanerch, where it divides. Take left-hand turning and follow old road for ½ mile to where path turns straight up hillside to Carn Edward. Follow this path, and walk left along ridge for ¾ mile to Mynydd Caregog (1,021 ft.), where four tracks meet. Take the one (right-hand) that leads north. Half a mile farther on you strike the road to NEWPORT. Turn right for ¾ mile along this road until you see an old track to the right which leads you down the hillside into the town. (From Newport take bus to reach Cardigan, the nearest railway.)

Distance 14 miles.

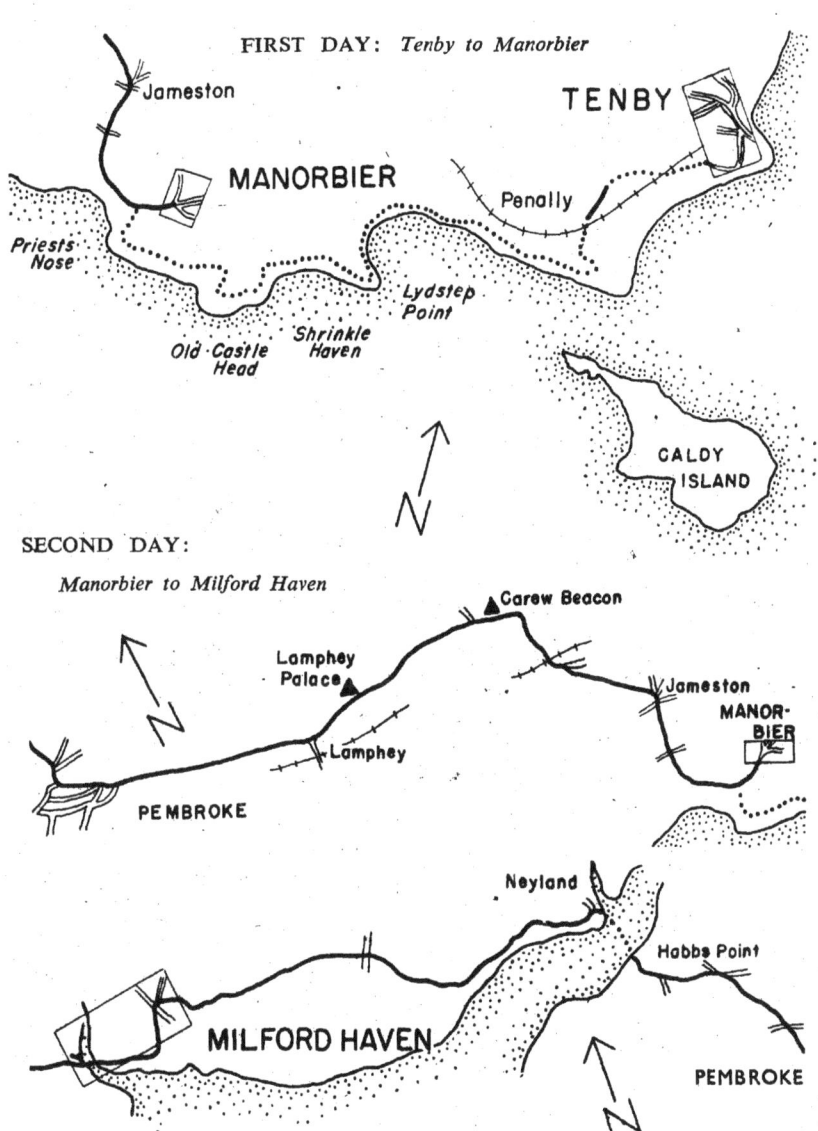

THIRD DAY: *Milford Haven to Little Haven*

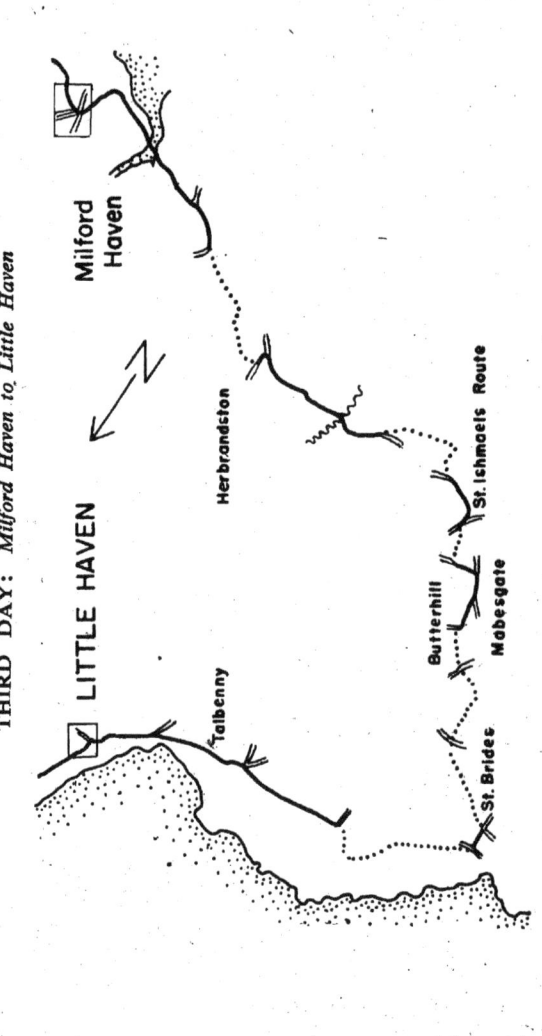

FOURTH DAY: Little Haven to St. Davids

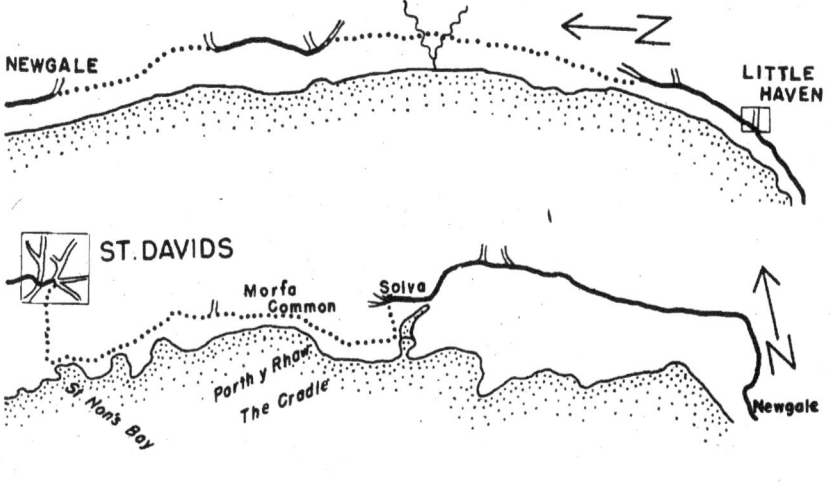

FIFTH DAY: St. Davids to Trevine

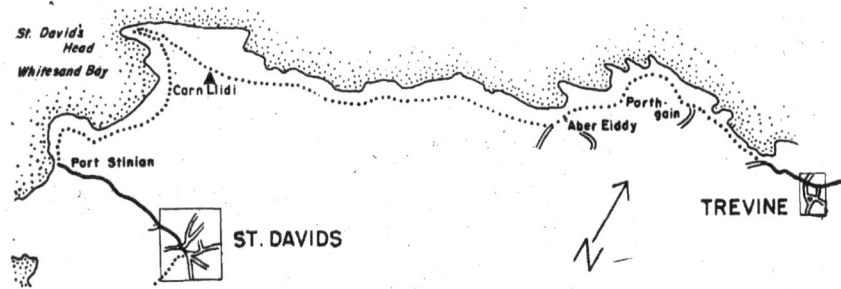

SIXTH DAY: *Trevine to Fishguard*

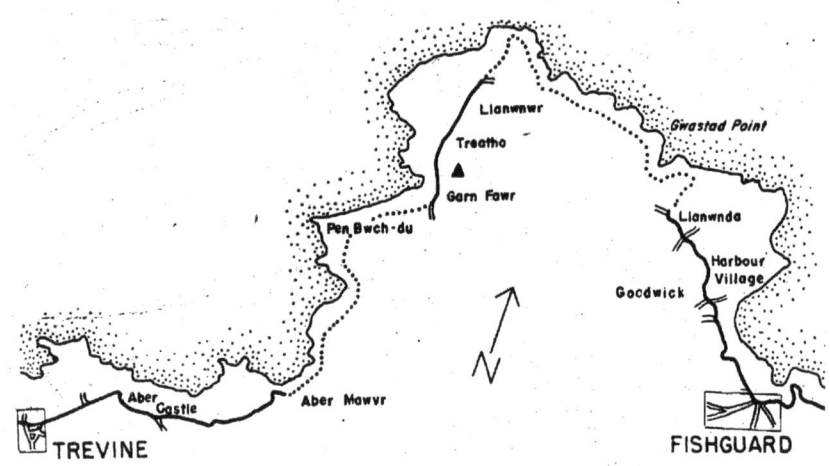

SEVENTH DAY: *Fishguard to Newport*

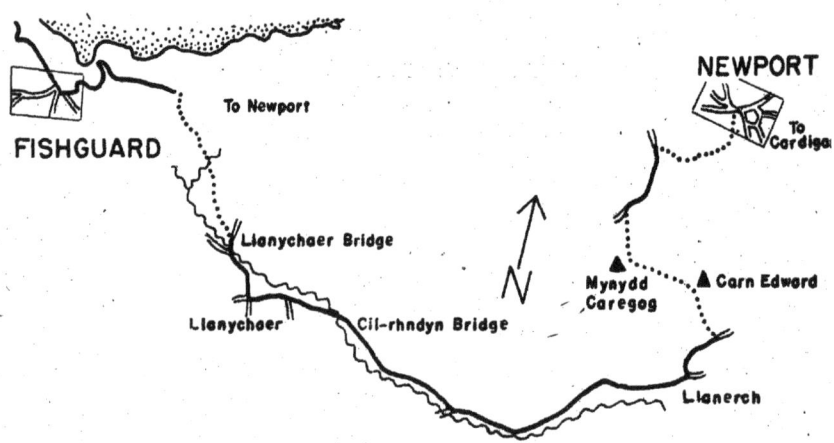

7. SMUGGLERS' COAST—THE LIZARD PENINSULA

Falmouth Bay and the Carrick Roads possess a landscape of shelving rocks, wooded estuaries and rivers, picturesque Cornish villages and an almost sub-tropical vegetation, which would be difficult to match elsewhere in England; for this district traps the sun, yet feels the cool sea breezes—and above all it contains the lovely name of St. Anthony-in-Roseland. In absolute contrast is the Lizard Peninsula, with the grandeur of its grim coastline—a coast notorious in the past for its shipwreckers and smugglers.

Note.—This is a strenuous tour, especially that part which takes you round the coastline of the Lizard Peninsula. Much of the walking has to be done along coastguard paths, and coastguards seem to patrol too little, for many of these paths are rough and stony—and steep. Still, you will be well repaid for your exertions. Three " tips " for the hiker in Cornwall:

Don't criticise the strange, medieval superstitions of many of the local inhabitants, which are still believed in;

Get a liking for the enormous Cornish pasties; and

Don't put too much reliance in the signposts. Cornwall is the worst-signposted area in England, and many of the signposts you come upon point the wrong way—they are meant, I think, to deceive the " piskies "!

Summary of distances

1. Truro to Veryan	. . . . .	12 miles
2. Falmouth	. . . . . .	10 ,,
3. Manaccan	. . . . . .	10 ,,
4. Coverack	. . . . . .	12 ,,
5. Lizard	. . . . . .	12 ,,
6. Mullion	. . . . . .	12 ,,
7. Helston	. . . . . .	12 ,,
Total Distance	. . . . .	80 ,,

Train travel
  Truro and Helston. G.W.R.

Bus travel
  Western National Omnibus Co., Ltd

Maps
  One-inch Ordnance Survey, sheets 143, 146.

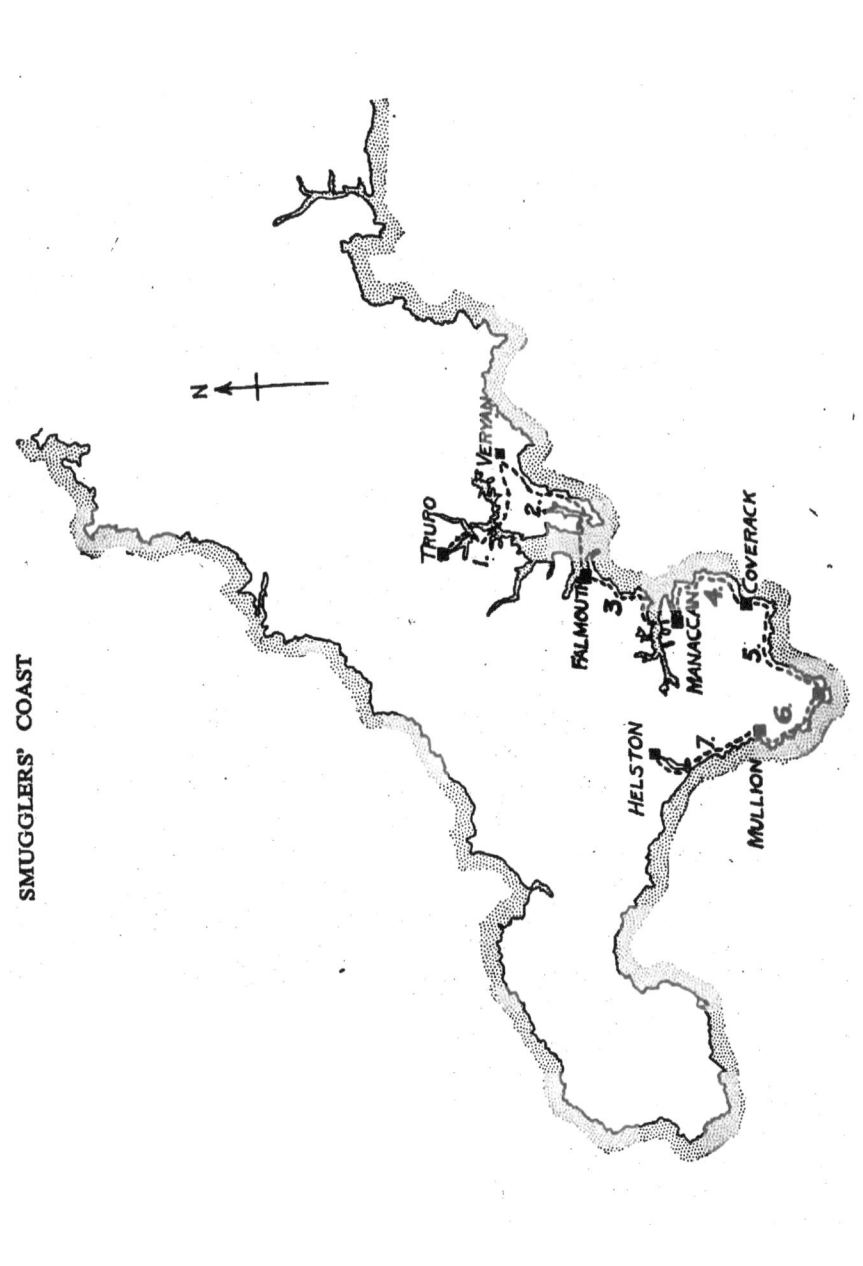

FIRST DAY

Truro is an old riverside city, dominated by first English provincial cathedral built since the Reformation. Leave Truro by riverside road for Malpas (pronounced " Mopus "), 2 miles. Malpas is in exquisitely wooded country, and this extends down the River Fal to Feock. At Malpas (inn) cross by boat to reach Old Kea (Kea being an Irish saint). Now take the only road inland for a mile to a junction. Turn right ¼ mile, then left, and continue south for 1½ miles until you reach the ferry road. Turn left through woodland to the hamlet of Trelissick, where you get the ferry. The King Harry whose name gives the passage a touch of romance is Henry VIII, who is reputed to have stayed the night at Trelissick on his way to inspect the site of Pendennis Castle. A ¼ mile inland a right-hand road runs through lovely scenery to St. Just-in-Roseland, but your route goes straight ahead for 3 miles to Philleigh, and then another 2½ miles until you reach a main road. Turn right, then left to the long, scattered village of VERYAN. The two strange, thatched round-houses at either end of the village are known as " Parson Trust's Houses ". They are reputed to keep the devil out of Veryan! A pleasant stroll can be made down to the wild and magnificent coast at Portloe.

Distance 12 miles.

SECOND DAY

From Veryan take the Gerrans road (it is possible, but rough going, to follow the sea-coastal path). By road you pass under the shoulder of the strikingly sudden hill known as Carn Beacon. It is a hill upon a hill. On the left-hand side of the road, just before entering Trewithian, is Dingerein Castle, an ancient earthwork. At Trewithian take the left-hand road to Gerrans (like many other Cornish place-names this place is named after an obscure saint). There is a magnificent view here from the churchyard. If you have time, make a short

SMUGGLERS' COAST—THE LIZARD

detour to the pleasant little seaside resort of Portscatho. Following the scenic road on for over 3 miles, you finally arrived at St. Anthony-in-Roseland. It is perhaps a pity to disillusion the reader but "roseland" actually stands for "rossland" or heath. You now cross the water by boat to St. Mawes and thence to FALMOUTH—a somewhat uninteresting town. If you have the time and inclination, there are frequent trips by steamer up the Carrick Roads. St. Just-in-Roseland is well worth such a visit, if only to see the church standing delightfully by the water's edge, and the perfect churchyard, shaped like a bowl, and a veritable garden of sub-tropical plants and flowers.

Distance 10 miles.

THIRD DAY

As Falmouth is long and straggly, I suggest you take a bus to Swanpool Beach, and there take to a path across the golf-links to Maen Porth. From there follow the road or the coast-path to Mawnan, a remote village, standing at the entrance of the Helford River. From Mawnan proceed to the ferry near Durgan which takes you to Helford. This is a charming, rustic village, lying in a deep hollow. It can be very hot and steamy, but this results in a profusion of flowers, geraniums running over the thatch and fronts of most of the houses. Now make the climb up to MANACCAN, which sits on the hilltop. As this has been a fairly short day, you may wish to visit St. Anthony-in-Meneage, where there is an interesting and beautifully situated twelfth-century church on Gillian Creek. From here you get a splendid view of Falmouth Bay. Or you can combine this with your next day's walk.

Distance 10 miles.

FOURTH DAY

From Manaccan you emerge into the true Lizard country. It is best, although strenuous, to follow the cliff-walk most of the way. Inland lies the vast Goonhilly Downs, which are not interesting except to botanists and archaeologists. For sheer bleakness these downs are hard to beat, despite a certain charm during the flowering of the heath. So make your way to the coast near Nare Point and follow the coast-path to Porthallow (inn). Two miles farther on is Porthoustock. Half a mile farther on you look out on the Manacles, the most murderous rocks on a murderous coast. Dreaded by seafarers they are not obtrusive to the visitor, for their danger lies beneath the surface of the water. There have been some terrible wrecks on these rocks, some of them in the past engineered by the piratical villagers of St. Keverne. The name "Manacle" is derived from the Cornish "maen eglos", meaning "church stone". I cannot tell why. St. Keverne is reached by road. Its church, a landmark, is one of the few in Cornwall that has a spire instead of a square tower. In the churchyard are several memorials to those sailors who were lost in wrecks. From St. Keverne I followed a path and track that went due south over lonely country to the coast, and a mile farther on brought me to COVERACK. Let me say here that in the Lizard I consider the carrying of a compass essential. What signposts there are one finds are often incorrect, and should a sudden fog or mist descend it is easy to get "lost"—a most unpleasant dilemma. Coverack is one of the most delightful seaside spots in all Cornwall. In the past it was possibly the most popular smuggling centre in the whole Lizard. To-day bathing, boating and fishing are the attractions.

Distance 12 miles.

FIFTH DAY

This is a stiff day, with most of the going along the cliffs. From Coverack make for Black Head. You now see the famed serpentine rock, which continues right round the coast as far as Mullion. From Black Head it is strenuous up-and-down walking until Kennack Sands are reached. Here you find the only sandy foreshore for miles. Thorny Cliff has now to be tackled, and its name is highly suited, for there are many thorny brambles to slow your pace, and the path (!) is largely

SMUGGLERS' COAST—THE LIZARD

loose stones. I would almost suggest walking to Poltesco by road, and from there a ½ mile climb brings you to Ruan Minor, which is a pretty village with an interesting church. A steep descent for ½ mile brings you to Cadgwith, where the sea comes hissing in to the "Devil's Fryingpan". Another steep ascent and a good mile's walk brings you to Church Cove. Here you take a lovely tree-shaded lane to Landewendack. You pass houses embowered with roses and honeysuckle, like a conservatory and a strange contrast to the windswept barren heath beyond. Landewendack has the most southerly church in England, and it was here the last sermon in the Cornish language was preached in 1674. Half a mile on by road is LIZARD (town), an uninteresting, haphazard sort of place, whose population is chiefly engaged in working up curios from the serpentine stone.

Distance 12 miles.

SIXTH DAY

Lizard Point is ¾ mile south of Lizard town. It is the most southerly point of England and is the first sight of English soil which many people coming to England get. Lizard has nothing to do with reptiles, but is the Cornish for "rocky heights". From here walk along the cliff to Pentreath Beach and Kynance Cove. You pass Postal Meadow with its mounds of 700 dead, taken from a wrecked transport from which only two men were saved. Strangely enough, nothing is known of the name of the ship or the date of its being wrecked. The beauties of Kynance Cove can only be observed at low tide, when the wonderful colour of the multi-tinted serpentine rocks, stuck in the yellow sand, and the green-blue translucent sea and sunny sky make a perfect picture. Beyond Kynance Cove is the strange-looking Asparagus Island (but no asparagus). It can be reached by the nimble-footed. Here you find the "Devil's Post-office", where you can post a "letter" with astonishing results! Continuing on by coastguard path, the hiker finds himself amidst black and savage grandeur—alone with the gulls and rabbits. Inland lies Predannack Downs, which I knew full well, for it was a war-time airfield—a Godforsaken spot. In due course you arrive at Mullion Cove, with its tiny, delightful harbour, Porth Mellin. Let us hope you see it on a fine day, when it gives a possibly deceptive appearance of calm. During the autumn and winter gales giant waves, hungry for power, seem to seize it. In the neighbourhood have been many wrecks, and smuggling was, as usual, an important local industry. To-day a number of high-class hotels are established here. MULLION lies inland over a mile. The church has interest, and some fine bench-ends.

Distance 12 miles.

SEVENTH DAY

Leaving behind the hotels and ".civilization" of Mullion, make for the coast again at Polurrian Cove. A coastguard path runs to Poldhu Cove. It was at Poldhu that Marconi in 1901 sent the first wireless message across to America. A fairly easy walk brings you to Gunwalloe Church standing lonely beside the seashore, a church but no village, and dedicated to St. Winwaloe, a medieval Breton saint (Gunwalloe is a perversion of his name). In this neighbourhood there were more shipwrecks than anywhere else, and vast treasures are reputed to be buried under the sands of the sea. Ascending from Gunwalloe the track skirts Halsferran Cliff, and thence you descend to Loe Bar, which encloses Loe Pool, 7 miles in circumference and the only real lake in Cornwall. This bar was formed, so local legend claims, when a dishonest steward, one Tregeagle, condemned to carry sacks, containing sand, to Porthleven, was tripped up by a demon— and the bar created! A path will lead you to the Porthleven-Helston road. Two miles farther on is HELSTON, famous for its annual "Furry Dance" held on May 8. You may appreciate better its excellent local "Home-brewed " ale.

Distance 12 miles.

FIRST DAY: *Truro to Veryan*

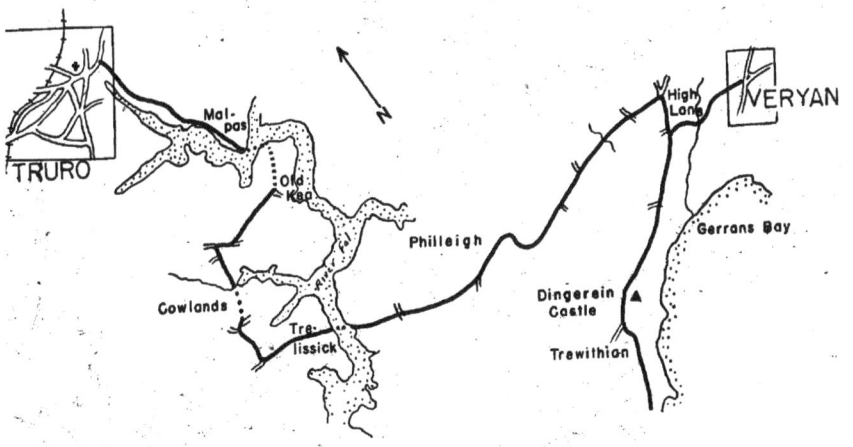

SECOND DAY: *Veryan to Falmouth*

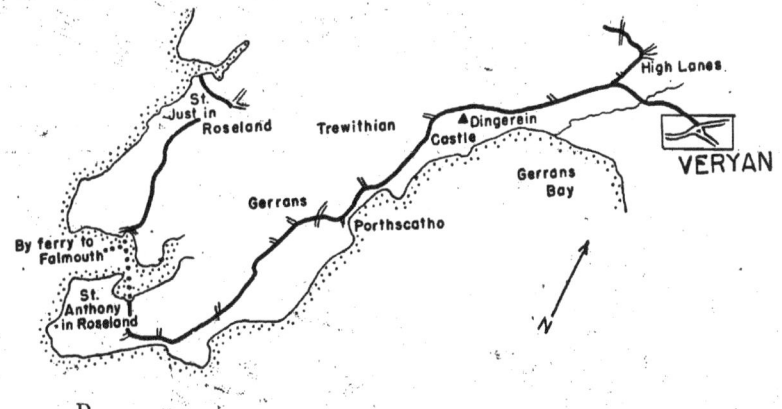

D

FALMOUTH

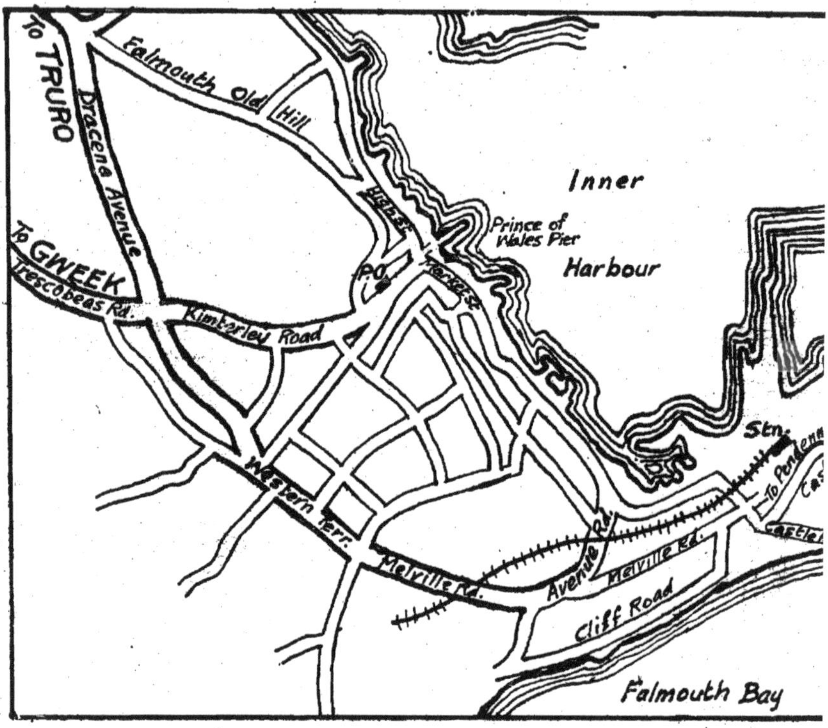

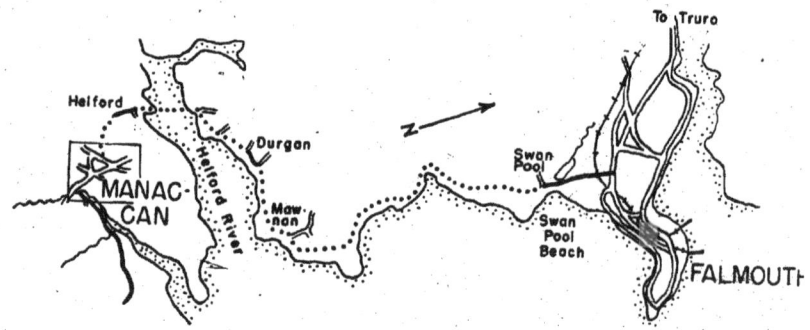

THIRD DAY: *Falmouth to Manaccan*

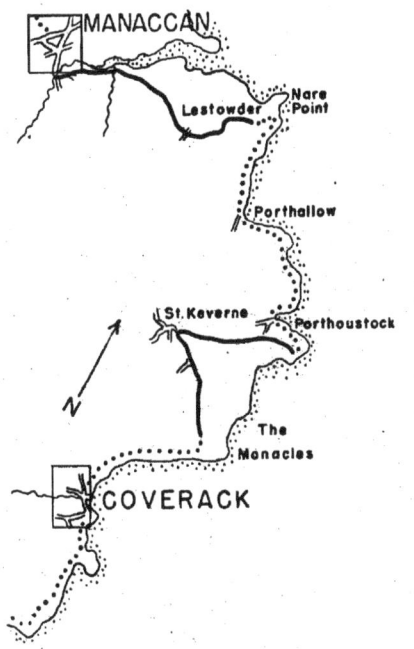

FOURTH DAY: *Manaccan to Coverack*

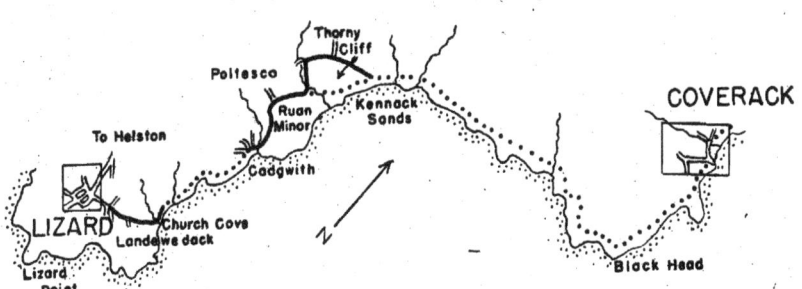

FIFTH DAY: *Coverack to Lizard*

SIXTH DAY: *Lizard to Mullion*

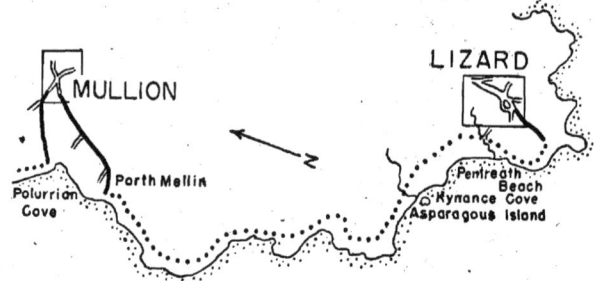

SEVENTH DAY: *Mullion to Helston*

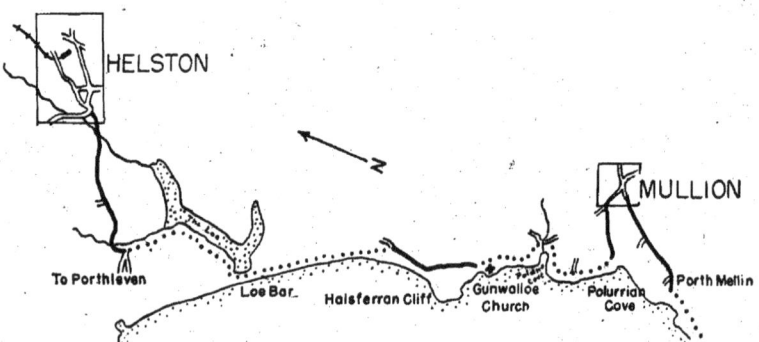

8. FROM DUNKERY TO TINTAGEL

Dunster, Dunkery, Selworthy and Porlock make a splendid opening to a walking tour which is, I think, my favourite one. It is strenuous, for there is much scrambling up and down coastguard paths, but there is no monotony, as each successive point seems to bring even more lovely views of coast scenery. There is, also, the wild heath of Exmoor, wooded valleys and waterfalls, and towns like Barnstaple and Bideford, romantically linked with the Spanish Main. Then comes the calm and peace of Clovelly, quaintest of villages, to be followed by the breathless exhilaration of the wild coastline between Hartland Point and Tintagel, over which all the gales of heaven seem to sweep.

Summary of distances

1. MINEHEAD TO PORLOCK . . . . 15 miles
2. LYNMOUTH . . . . . . 16 ,,
3. ILFRACOMBE . . . . . . 16 ,,
4. BARNSTAPLE (or BIDEFORD) . . . 12 ,,
5. HARTLAND QUAY . . . . . 12 ,,
6. BUDE . . . . 12 ,,
7. TINTAGEL . . . . . . 16 ,,

    Total Distance: . . . . . 99 ,,

Train travel
Minehead. G.W.R.
Camelford. S.R.

Bus travel
Western National Omnibus Co., Ltd.
Southern National Omnibus Co., Ltd.

Maps
One-inch Ordnance Survey, sheets 119, 118, 127, 136.

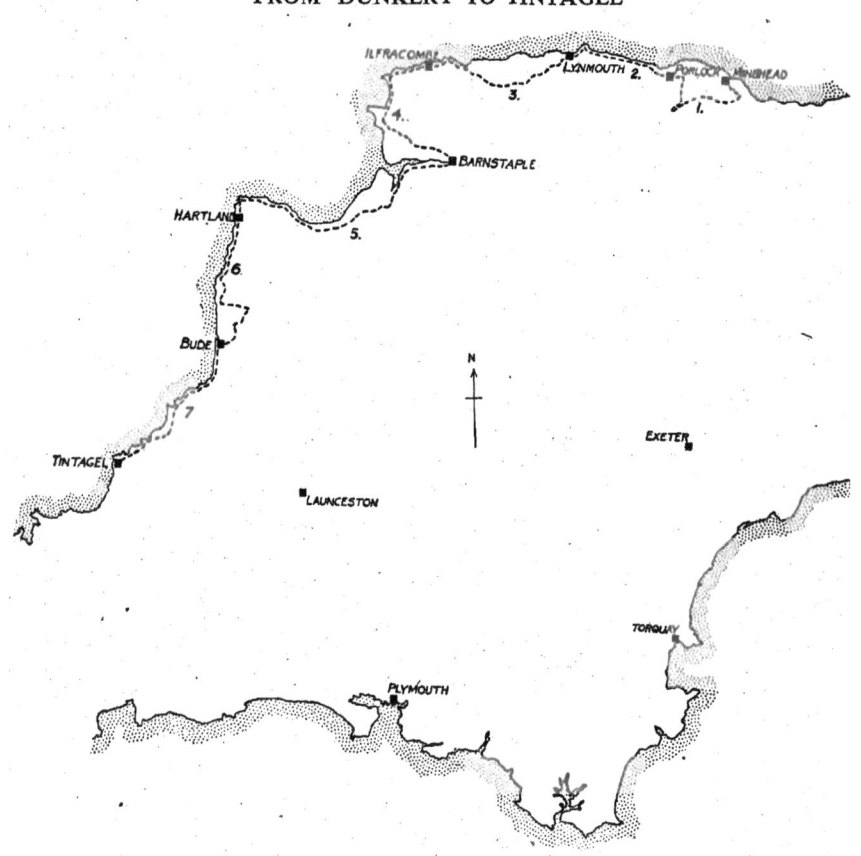

FIRST DAY

From Minehead walk or take bus to Dunster, a most picturesque village, with its castle, still held by the Luttrell family, who have lived there since 1376, an interesting church, a quaint street with an ancient yarn-market building, and the Luttrell Arms, one of England's famous historic inns. From Dunster turn right on the moorland road to Wooton Courtney, a charming and remote village. From here you follow on to Dunkery Beacon (1,707 ft.), from which you get a magnificent view. Strike down hill to Luccombe, a little village enshrouded in flowers, and from there bear left on a road which links up with the main Minehead-Porlock road. You turn right here for $\frac{1}{4}$ mile, and then left to Selworthy, a real gem, belonging to the National Trust. Do not miss the church, from which you get a splendid view. Now return to the main road again, and walk or bus on to PORLOCK, an exquisite village enclosed by hills except on the seaward side. It also is a bower of flowers.

Distance 15 miles.

SECOND DAY

From Porlock take the road to Porlock Weir. Turn off the seafront behind The Anchor, and follow first the road and then the track, through woods, up to Culbone, a village of two houses and the smallest church in England. Notice the unusual names on some of the tombstones. Continue on by path, often through woods, until you reach Glenthorne, a lonely house, lying on the boundary of Somerset and Devon. Disregard various notice-boards regarding " Trespassers will be prosecuted ". You won't be able, however, to disregard the stings of horse-flies which seem very prevalent in the woods. Four miles from Glenthorne you rise to Foreland Point (1,000 ft.), with its lighthouse and a view which on fine days embraces seven or eight counties. (Locally they say when you do get this clear view it foretells rainy weather.) From Foreland Point you start on a precipitous descent to Countisbury (inn) and on to LYNEMOUTH, a wonderful seaside beauty spot, with very narrow streets, romantically cradled in the mouth of a gorge hemmed in by steep, luxuriantly wooded hills.

Distance 16 miles.

THIRD DAY

By steep path (or cliff railway) ascend to Lynton, a popular holiday resort. Now follow the North Walk, along a path of great beauty, past huge jutting crags, until you bend left and enter the Valley of Rocks. Here is an indescribable wildness, no vegetation, and enormous masses of granite. Follow the road leading down the valley to Wringcliff Bay, overhung with a ferny precipice. Now on to Lee Bay, perhaps the loveliest of all bays on this coast. On your right before reaching Lee Bay is Duty Point, locally known as " Jennifred's Leap ". On again along delightful lanes round the shore of Woody Bay, through woods with here and there a waterfall—an idyllic scene. A road the far side of the bay leads you up to Hunter's Inn, and from here I suggest you follow the road, over the wild, windy waste of Trentishoe and Holdstone Downs (over 1,000 ft.) to Combe Martin. It is possible to follow the almost inaccessible paths along the coast from Heddon Mouth to Great Hangman's Point, but it is most exhausting. Combe Martin is a long-spun-out village, 1¼ miles long. It has an interesting church and a most unusual-looking inn, The Pack of Cards. The story goes that a long-dead squire once won a fortune at the card-table, and erected this building out of his gains. The house has fifty-two windows (the number of cards in a pack), and is interesting inside. In the Middle Ages Combe Martin had a prosperous silver-mining industry, but to-day vegetable-growing is the main industry. During the season strawberries are produced in great quantities. The road to Ilfracombe winds round Combe Martin Bay, rising and falling abruptly. It follows close to the coast. ILFRACOMBE is unusually situated, and is a popular holiday resort—a complete contrast to the lonely miles you have travelled during the day.

Distance 16 miles.

FOURTH DAY.

From Ilfracombe take the clearly defined cliff path through Torrs Wood for 2 miles to Lee (inn). From here you descend into the "Valley of Fuschias", a wonderful sight when in flower. Passing across some beautiful combes the road passes the golf-links on the left to reach Bull Point. From there follows a lovely 2-mile walk along a private road to the village of North Morte, or you can follow the coast-path around Rockham Bay to Morte Point, a beautiful headland, not grim as the name might suggest to landsmen, but highly dangerous and dreaded by mariners. The Point is now the property of the National Trust. In the neighbourhood is a number of prehistoric burial chambers. The near-by village of Mortehoe is a desolate-looking collection of houses, but the church contains in its peal the oldest bell in England. A long steep road brings you down to Woolacombe, plagued with many ugly boarding-houses, for the place is a tourist resort. The scenery now changes, and for 2 miles you have an easy walk alongside the golf-links and thence on to Croyde. If you wish, you can make a detour to Baggy Point with its wild cliffs. Croyde is a rustic village, situated in a valley that runs down to the sea. From Croyde to Barnstaple I suggest taking bus, although a visit *en route* to St. Brannock's church, near Braunton, is well worth making. On the right-hand side of the road is a great airfield which during the war held the record score for submarines destroyed by Coastal Command. BARNSTAPLE is an ancient and historic seaport, with a wealth of old houses associated with Elizabethan merchant-princes. At that time Spanish coins circulated more freely in the town than those bearing Elizabeth's head. The church is very beautiful.

Distance 12 miles (to Croyde).

FIFTH DAY

From Barnstaple take bus to Bideford with its famous bridge and its connection with Charles Kingsley, who wrote *Westward Ho!* here. A visit to Westward Ho! itself is scarcely necessary, for it is a depressing spot. Instead take the Clovelly bus and get off at Hobby Lodge. Here, on payment of a small fee, you can take the lovely Hobby Drive to Clovelly (2½ miles). From this winding road you get the finest peeps of the sea-coast and also over to Lundy, that rather extraordinary island which is still a private " kingdom " and the home of thousands of puffins. Clovelly is wonderful and unique, and you may find it difficult to tear yourself away from it. When you do you turn past the churchyard into a farmyard, then left, then right, and you follow a well-defined path to Gallantry Bower. For the next 6 miles you have a lot of scrambling to do to reach Hartland Point. The going is not easy, but the fine scenery is your reward. And you seem to have the world to yourself in this wild country which culminates in Hartland Point. Once round the bend you notice the fury of the Atlantic, especially during stormy weather. Now take a track to Blegberry Farm and on to Stoke Church, " The Cathedral of North Devon ", whose tower is a landmark for miles around. It is well worth a visit. Three-quarters of a mile to the sea brings you to HARTLAND QUAY, whose harbour has long disappeared, but which possesses one of the best hotels in England (I refer to its all-round hospitality, for the prices are reasonable). It is one of my favourite " escapist " haunts. It lies at the foot of the cliff, close to the sea, and when a storm is on I know no place more thrilling.

Distance 12 miles.

SIXTH DAY

From Hartland Quay you follow the coast path for over 10 miles. First you pass Speke's Mouth with its dramatic waterfall. Then, fairly easy going until you reach Welcombe Mouth. A steep hill separates you from Marsland Mouth, where you cross the border into Cornwall. After some more up-and-down scrambling you come to the Henna Cliff (450 ft.). The cliffs here are tremendous, sheer in places. On your left, inland ½ mile, stands Morwenstow Church, renowned for its

FROM DUNKERY TO TINTAGEL

singular poet-vicar, the Rev. R. S. Hawker ("and shall Trelawney die?"). Visit the church. Near-by is an eccentric-looking vicarage, but Hawker, who built it, was an eccentric. During service he liked cats and dogs to attend! At baptisms he used to pinch the infants to make them squeal and thus let the devil out! There is an inn close to the church. If you feel you have done enough scrambling, I suggest your taking the quiet road that leads south to Combe. Half a mile out of Morwenstow, Tanacombe, an interesting old manor-house, lies on your right. Combe lies in a charming ravine, but possibly equally welcome will be the tea you can obtain there. From Combe you can walk up the valley through woods to Kilkhampton, an uninteresting place, and from there take bus to Bude. The coastal scenery from Combe to Bude is rather an anticlimax to what has gone before. BUDE is another popular holiday resort.

Distance 12 miles (to Combe).

SEVENTH DAY

As you have a long day before you, I suggest taking the bus to Widemouth, otherwise take the coast path until you strike the coast road about a mile from Bude. Then on to Widemouth Sand. Two miles farther on is Milhook Haven, the only place in Britain you find the rare "Plymouth Blue" butterfly. From Milhook you have steep climbing to reach Dizzard Point, but there is also a succession of scenic surprises. At Cleave there is the usual deep-wooded valley and stream, and the inevitable scrambling climb. St. Gennys, named after its patron saint, St. Genesius (legend claims the saint bowed to the executioner after he had been beheaded, and then picked up his head and walked off with it tucked under his arm!), is close to Crackington Haven, a noble and lovely spot. Cambeak looms ahead, but by-pass it and strike across 2 miles over the shoulder of the down to High Cliff (731 ft.), where you see more savage cliffs, and then by rough road to Pentargan Bay. From here take a steep road down to Boscastle, with its tiny land-locked harbour, and romantically situated in a deep ravine. You have your choice of the Wellington Hotel at one end of a mile-long street and the Napoleon Inn at the other. Close to Boscastle harbour is a ghastly chasm near the Blackapit. There is a coastal path from Boscastle to Tintagel, 4 miles distant. After your long walk, however, you may favour the main road which passes Trevalga (its name is unchanged since Domesday), Rocky Valley, and Bossiney (until 1832 this tiny place returned two members to Parliament. Sir Francis Drake was once its representative). Finally, you arrive at Tintagel, celebrated for its Arthurian associations, but now much developed as a popular holiday resort. You may find TINTAGEL a disappointment. Take bus to Camelford for train connection.

Distance 16 miles.

FIRST DAY: *Minehead to Porlock*

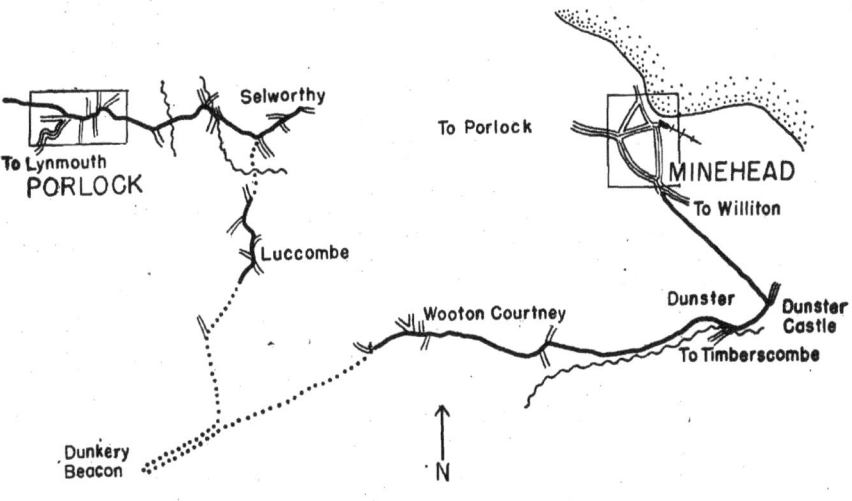

SECOND DAY: *Porlock to Lynmouth*

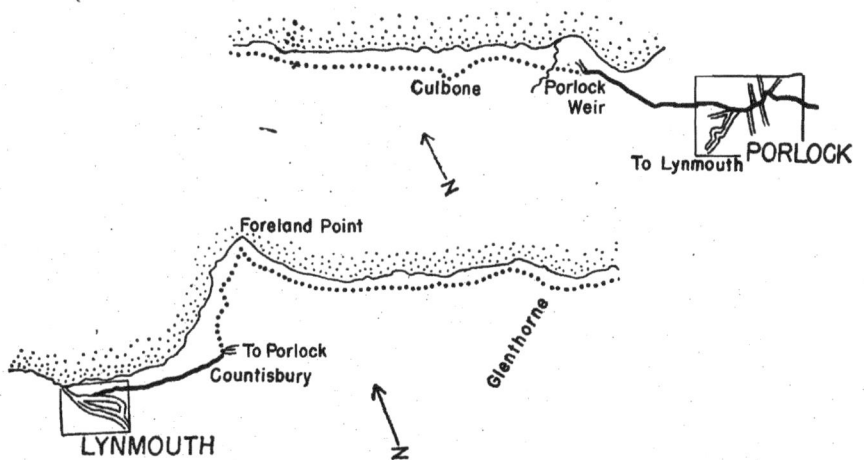

THIRD DAY: *Lynmouth to Ilfracombe*

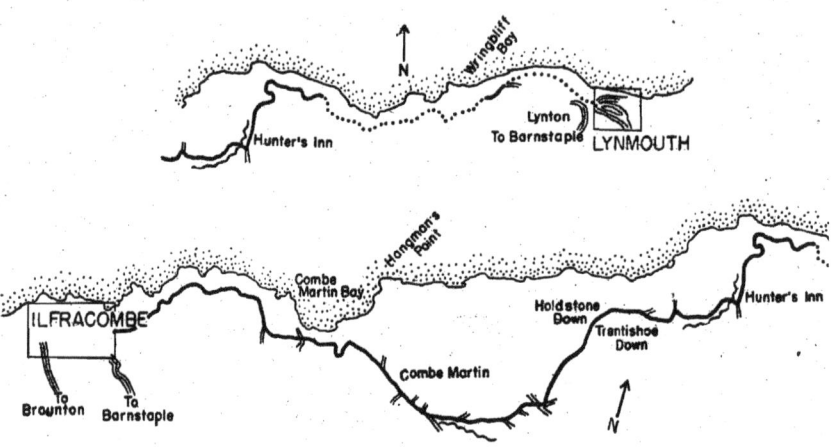

FOURTH DAY: *Ilfracombe to Barnstaple*

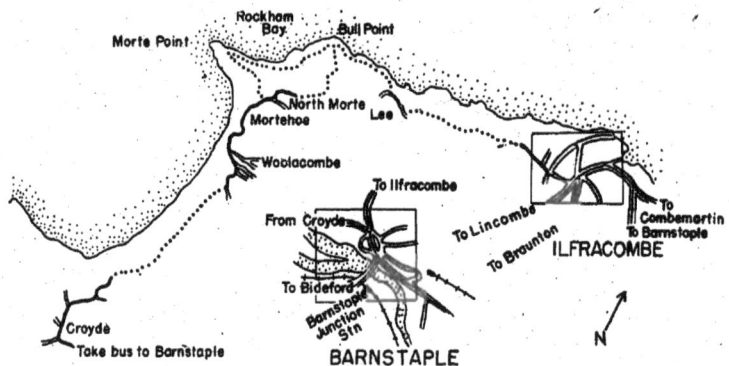

FIFTH DAY: *Barnstaple to Hartland Quay*

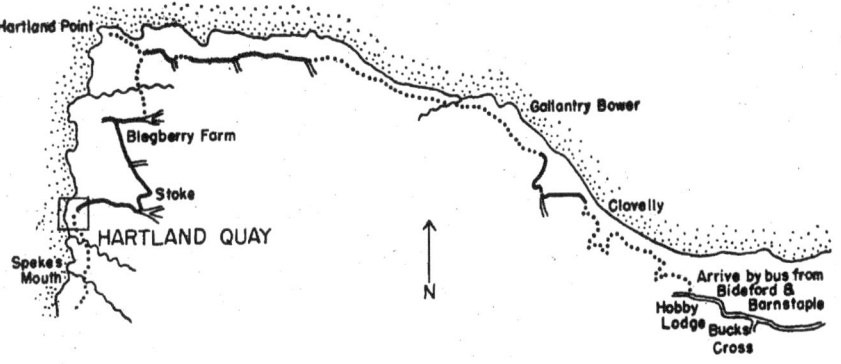

SIXTH DAY: *Hartland Quay to Bude*

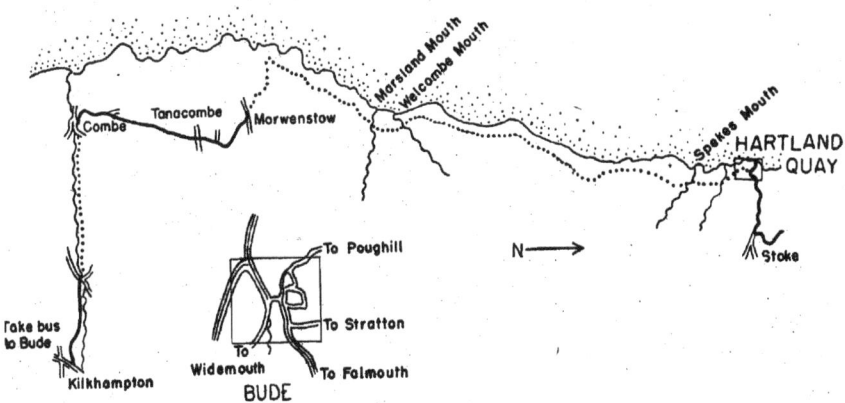

SEVENTH DAY: *Bude to Tintagel*

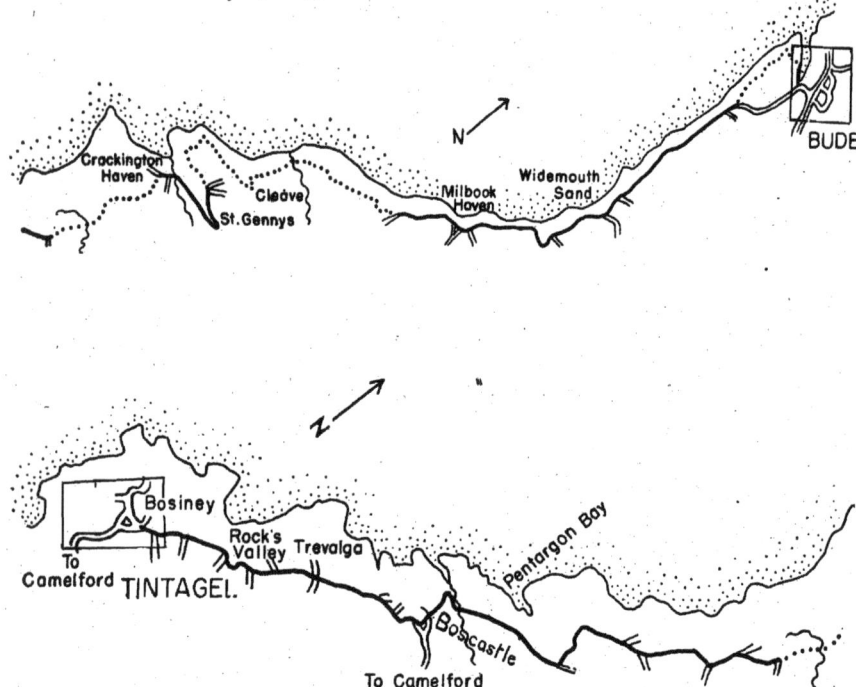

9. ENGLISH LAKELAND

The Lakes!—Who does not know, either by personal experience or by reputation, something of the glamour of this lovely corner of England? Is it necessary to tell of the many charms of this beautiful countryside—the high mountains towering into the sky; the long winding lakes with their green shores and islands, but each with its own peculiar attractions; the deep-wooded valleys; and, last but not least, the picturesque towns and villages with their wealth of literary and historical atmosphere.

The Youth Hostels are in good supply in this part of England, a useful point in a somewhat rainy area.

Summary of distances

1. KESWICK TO PATTERDALE . . . . 14 miles
2. GRASMERE . . . . . . 10 ,,
3. AROUND GRASMERE . . . . . 14 ,,
4. CONISTON . . . . . . 15 ,,
5. BOOT . . . . 15 ,,
6. BORROWDALE . . . . . . 15 ,,
7. KESWICK . . . . . . 9 ,,

       Total Distance . . . . . 92 ,,

Train travel
    Keswick. L.M.S.

Bus travel
    Ribble Motor Services, Ltd.
    Cumberland Motor Services, Ltd.

Maps
    One-inch Ordnance Survey, sheets 19 and 20.

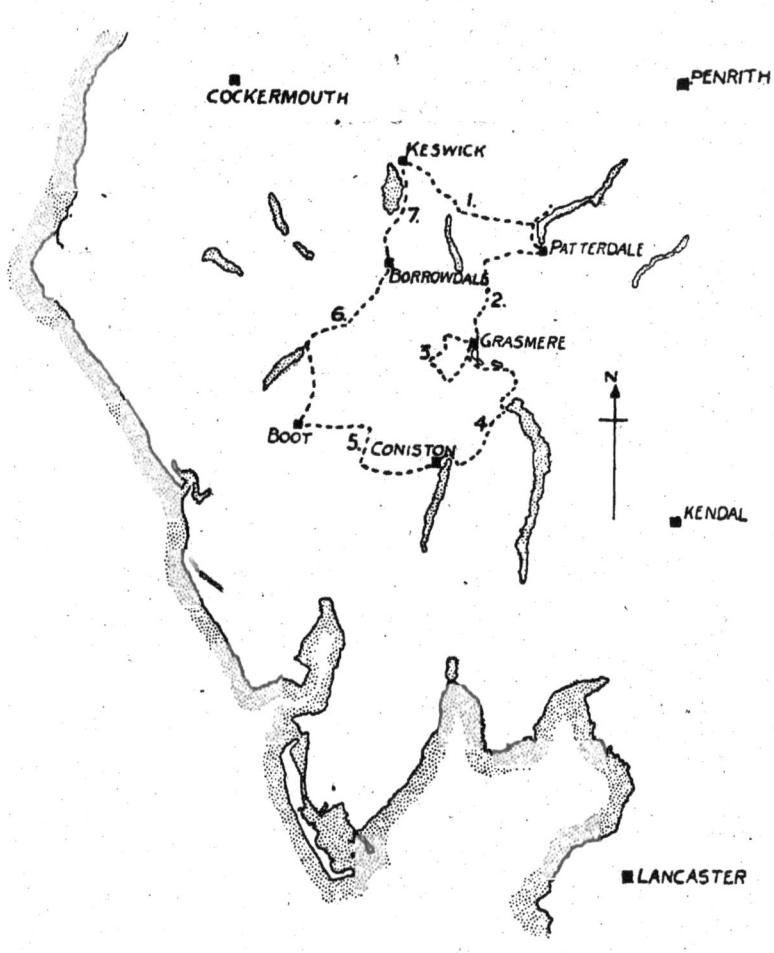

FIRST DAY

Keswick is pleasantly situated at the head of Derwentwater, and as "capital" of the Lake District has accommodation for every type of visitor. Several days could be spent here alone, exploring the lakeside on foot and the lake itself by boat, or in climbing the mountains which lie within a short walking distance: Bleaberry Fell, Cat Bells, Hobcarton End and Skiddaw.

For first day's journey walk or take bus $4\frac{1}{2}$ miles to Stybeck at the upper end of Thirlmere. There turn up path past Stanah Farm to Stanah Gill. Path climbs steeply up right-hand side of gill to shoulder of mountain (2,250 ft.), and marks entrance to Stighe Pass. The summit of pass is just under 2,500 feet, and gives a grand view over the mountains of central and western Lakeland. Path presently follows stream which flows into a small reservoir. Here track divides into three. Left-hand path goes to Dockray; right-hand goes downstream past Greenside Smelting Mills to the old road to Glenridding and Ullswater. We take the central path over short ridge below Sheffield Pike, which then drops down to Glencoyne Dale and skirts the hillside above the stream down to Glencoyne. Village overlooks the long winding lake of Ullswater. Before turning south along the road to Patterdale it is worth making a short detour north through Glencoyne Park to visit the waterfall of Aira Force. Returning to Glencoyne, proceed through Glencoyne Woods to Glenridding Bridge for PATTERDALE Village. Ullswater has been described as the noblest of the lakes. It is ringed round by high mountains and rocky crags, and some delightful days could be spent exploring its shores.

Distance 14 miles.

SECOND DAY

Of the various routes from Patterdale to Grasmere, one of the best-known is up Grisedale Beck to Grisedale Tarn, across

Grisedale Hause, and down Tongue Gill to the Grasmere-Keswick Road. But walkers who are attracted by the soaring bulk of Helvellyn may find the following way a pleasant alternative. Take side-road leading past Patterdale Hall up Grise Dale, and after ½ mile a lane will be met, bearing right across Grisedale Beck, with signpost marked " Helvellyn ". This track climbs steadily to 2,250 feet. At a gate near the end of Red Tarn the track divides. Both ways lead to the summit; the right-hand path goes by the easier route along Swirral Edge; the left-hand one by the more spectacular Striding Edge. In normal weather (i.e. fine weather) Striding Edge is not as dangerous as it may appear. It is certainly one of the finest ridge walks in the district. The view from the summit of Helvellyn (3,118 ft), is superb. Many of the well-known Lakeland mountains should be visible if the day is clear, as well as Cross Fell, Ingleborough and other Pennine summits. Solway Firth, Morecambe Bay and the various lakes are also visible.

From the summit follow path down along ridge for 1½ miles to Dollywagon Pike, where a steep descent of 1,000 feet leads to the north-eastern end of Grisedale Tarn and the track which is the direct route from Patterdale to Grasmere. Legend has it that hidden in the tarn is the magic crown of Dunmail, King of Cumbria, who ordered his followers to throw it into the lake after his defeat by the Saxons. The path curves round the south shore of the lake, traverses the pass of Grisedale Hause, and continues down Tongue Gill to the GRASMERE road. Lovers of Wordsworth will need no introduction to Grasmere, which has so many associations with his poems.

Distance 10 miles.

THIRD DAY

Grasmere is the centre of such a fascinating district that one day at least ought to be devoted to exploring the neighbourhood. So, to-day, let Langdale Pikes be our goal. From the village take the old lane and path leading up Easedale. Turn left where side valley comes down from Silver Howe to point marked 1,345 feet on Ordnance map. From there path bears right of stream, making steep descent to Pye Howe in Great Langdale Valley. The road can be followed up to the end of the valley with its grand views of the surrounding hills. The waterfall of Dungeon Ghyll Force can be seen up a side stream. From hotel take lane to Wall End, from where a minor road curves round Bles Tarn below Mart Crag and Busk Pike to Little Langdale Tarn. Pass road-turn on right and continue to Elterwater. Turn right at inn, where path will be seen going left up hill to main Grasmere-Langdales road. Turn right, and 100 yards on left is another path leading to foot of Red Bank by the shore of Grasmere. Follow the road along west side of lake back to GRASMERE.

Distance 14 miles.

FOURTH DAY

Retrace route skirting west side of lake to Red Bank. At bend of road a path continues along Loughrigg Terrace to picturesque Rydal Water and Rydal village. Keep clear of main road, but turn along secondary road leading down wooded Rothey Valley to Miller Bridge, where path will be seen leading to Ambleside. Ambleside's main attraction is Stockgill Force. Note curious house built on bridge over stream. Waterhead, ¾ mile away at the head of Lake Windermere, is the terminus for the steamer service around the lake. A journey by boat to Bowness and back gives a good opportunity for observing the beauties of the lake. Follow road to Coniston for ¾ mile, turn left at bridge along road leading through woods to Low Wray. A side-road leads to Wray Castle (National Trust), from which there is a grand view over Windermere. Continue along road ½ mile, and near end of Blelham Tarn a footpath will be seen turning right along tarn to White House. Follow lane 100 yards, turn left and footpath continues for a mile to road leading left into Hawkshead. This has been described as the " best little town in Lakeland ". Its picturesque houses, church, ancient hall, and Wordsworth associations certainly make it full of interest. Continue south along road for ¾ mile and turn right past School Wood along road leading over Hawkshead Moor, with its view of Esthwaite Water. After a mile a path will be seen going right over moor to a wooded dell, from which point it traverses Monk Coniston Moor, overlooking the head of Coniston Water. Descend to road by Hollin Bank, where road will be seen curving round head of lake to CONISTON.

Distance 15 miles.

FIFTH DAY

Near railway station commences an old road from Coniston to the Duddon Valley. The track skirts the slopes of Coniston Old Man and traverses the pass between Brown Pike and Walna Scar. From there it descends Long House Gill to Long House Farm, where a lane descends to the road running north to head of Duddon Valley. Continue north along road past Troutal to Hinning House, where old road continues north along River Duddon, through grand river scenery. The gorge through which the river runs at Birks Bridge is impressive. It is 2 miles to Cockley Beck Farm (718 ft.), where the route over Hard Knott Pass to the River Esk commences. The Pass is 1,281 feet high, and is reached by a zigzag route. Path follows old Roman road, and lower down Hardknott Castle can be seen. It is really the remains of a Roman fort with inn and temple nearby. Old road leads down more zigzags to River Esk, where a more modern road leads downstream to BOOT, 2 miles away.

Distance 15 miles.

SIXTH DAY

From inn a lane leads along right bank of Whillan Beck, skirting round Great Barrow to end of Eel Tarn, where track continues north over Eskdale Fell to Burnmoor Tarn. Track climbs to 977 feet, then descends to head of Wast Water. This is a deep, isolated lake in the midst of desolate mountain scenery. Cross bridge over Lingmell Beck to road leading

upstream to Wasdale Head, a remote hamlet surrounded by the towering heights of Yewbarrow, Kirk Fell, Lingmell and Scafell. The church claims to be one of the smallest in England.
Wasdale Head is a climbers' centre, and the ascent of Scafell Pikes (3,210 ft.) can be made from here. It is the highest summit in England. From the schoolhouse a track leads across stream to Lingmell Gill, continues upstream and along right-hand branch to Hollowstones, then by ridge between Lingmell summit and Scafell Pikes, where cairned track leads south-east to the top. The cairn on the summit is a memorial to the men of the Lake District who were killed in the First World War. From it there is a splendid view of the surrounding mountains. From it a track descends by Broad Crag to Esk Hause (2,490 ft.). Here track divides, turn left $\frac{3}{4}$ mile to Sprinkling Tarn. Track now goes down Grains Gill between the high peaks of Glaramara and Seathwaite Fell to Stockley Bridge.

If, on the other hand, you are content to worship mountains from afar and prefer leaving the climbing of them to others, take the route from Wasdale Head up Lingmell Beck to Sty Head, below the frowning precipices of Great Gable. Take path following west side of Styhead Tarn which leads down Styhead Gill to Stockley Bridge, where it joins the track from Scafell. Half a mile downstream is Seathwaite, said to be the wettest spot in England. From the village a road leads by the wooded banks of the Derwent to Seatoller and BORROWDALE.

Distance 15 miles.

SEVENTH DAY

From Borrowdale village follow Derwent downstream to Rosthwaite, a pretty hamlet of whitewashed cottages. A road and footpath proceed downhill to the head of Derwent Bay, by Castle Crag, the "Jaws of Borrowdale", to Grange and Keswick. A mile from Rosthwaite can be seen the celebrated Bowder Stone, a huge rock weighing 1,971 tons (the property of the National Trust). If you have time to spare, turn right at hotel, cross bridge over stream, and follow path leading to

Hazel Bank and Yew Crag to ridge overlooking Watendlath Tarn, with a grand view over the surrounding mountains. Cross ford over Watendlath Beck to Watendlath, a secluded hamlet with associations of Sir Hugh Walpole's Herries family. A rocky road leads down the valley to Ashness Bridge, a favourite viewpoint with artists and photographers. (Turn left to visit the Lodore Falls, of which Southey wrote—though be warned there is not much to see there except after heavy rains.) From the bridge to KESWICK is hardly 3 miles following the beautiful shores of the lake. The wooded promontory of Friar's Crag has been converted into a Ruskin Memorial.

Distance 9 miles.

FIRST DAY: *Keswick to Patterdale Village*

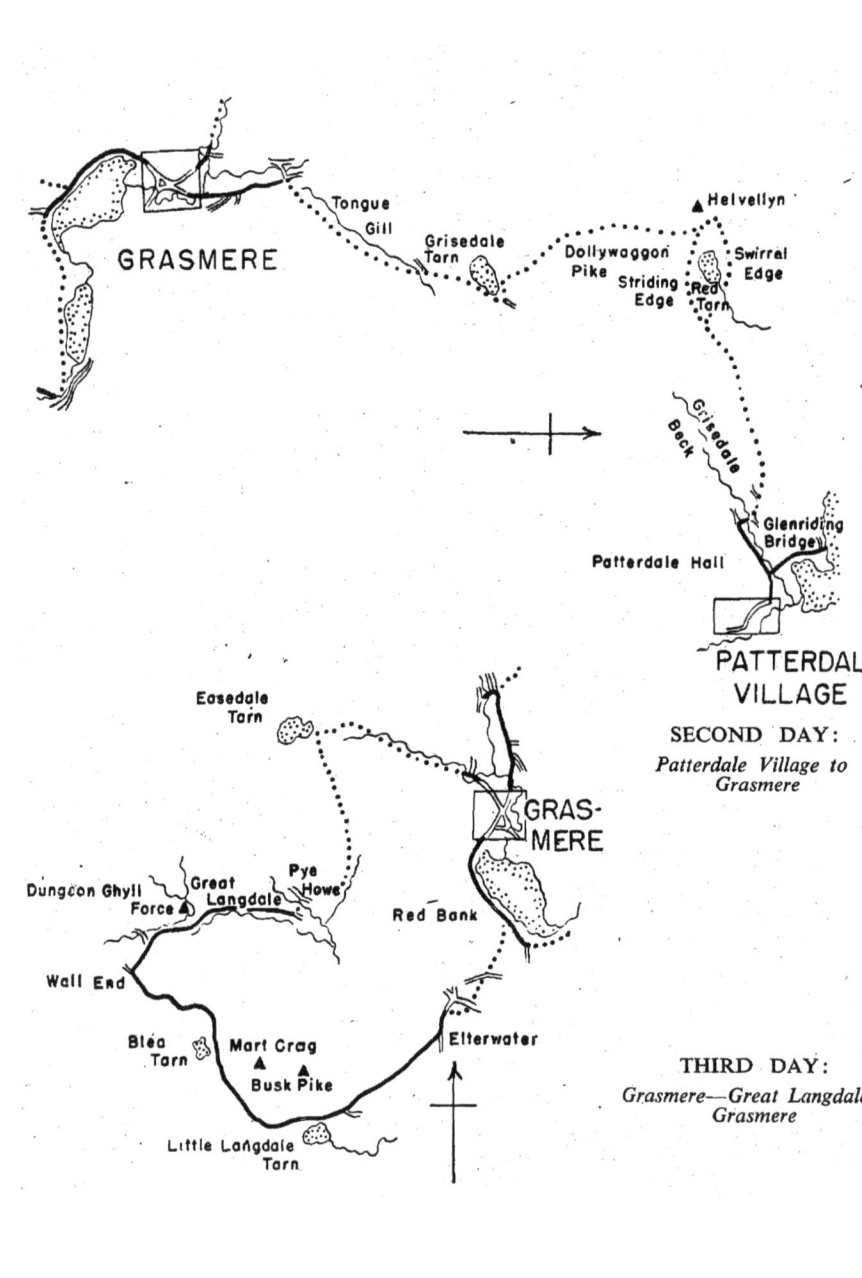

FOURTH DAY: *Grasmere to Coniston*

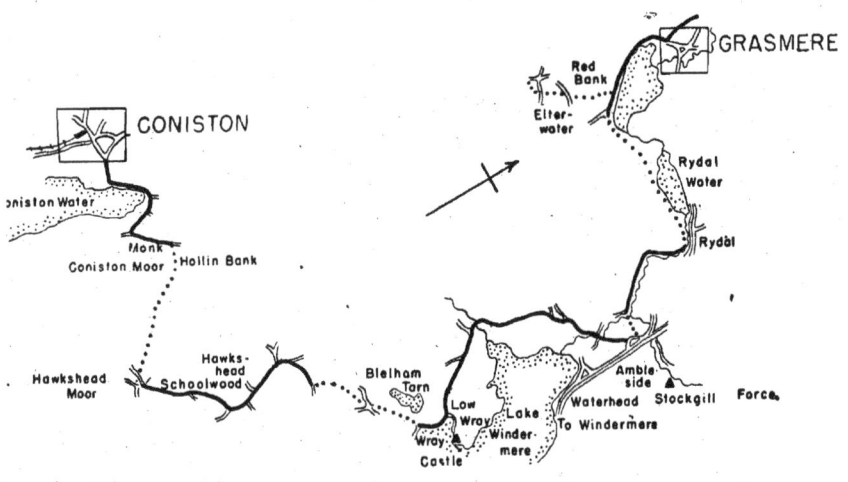

FIFTH DAY: *Coniston to Boot*

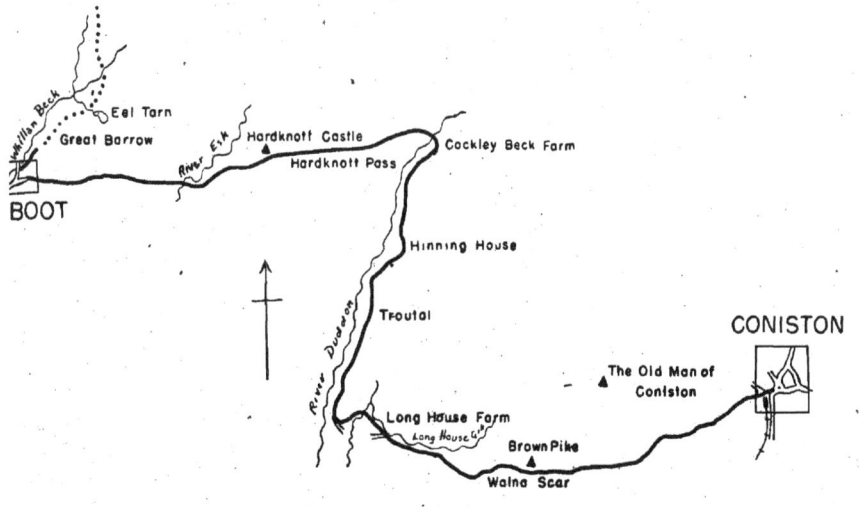

SIXTH DAY: *Boot to Borrowdale*

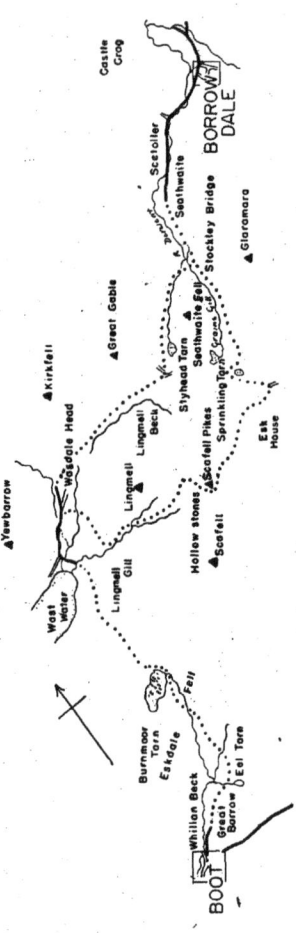

SEVENTH DAY: *Borrowdale to Keswick*

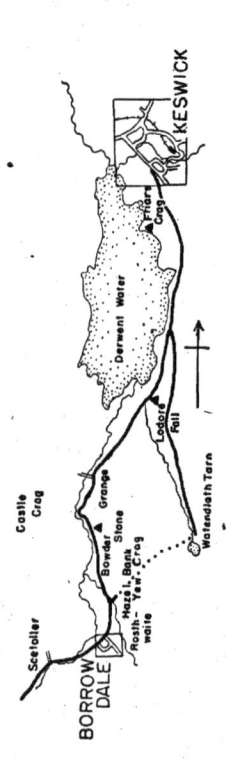

10. THE YORKSHIRE COAST

Yorkshire is not all dour moorlands or smoky industrial areas. Along the north-east coast stretches some of the finest cliff scenery in England. From Flamborough, where the gleaming white chalk cliffs rise sheer 400 feet from the blue sea, stretches a colourful, kaleidoscopic landscape of indented craggy bays and headlands. There are little wooded glens and picturesque old fishing-ports which can challenge comparison with any other stretch of coastline in Britain. One of the special joys of the itinerary given here is that it can be followed by footpath practically the whole of its length. Inland also are great sweeps of moorland and intimate little dales whose breath-taking beauty deserves to be better known.

Summary of distances

1. BRIDLINGTON TO FILEY	14	miles
2. SCARBOROUGH	9	,,
3. AROUND SCARBOROUGH	14	,,
4. ROBIN HOOD'S BAY	16	,,
5. WHITBY	8	,,
6. AROUND ESKDALE	14	,,
7. STAITHES	12	,,
Total Distance	87	,,

Train travel

Bridlington and Staithes. L.N.E.R.

Bus travel

East Yorkshire Motor Services, Ltd.

Maps

One-inch Ordnance Survey, sheets 23—16.

YORKSHIRE COAST

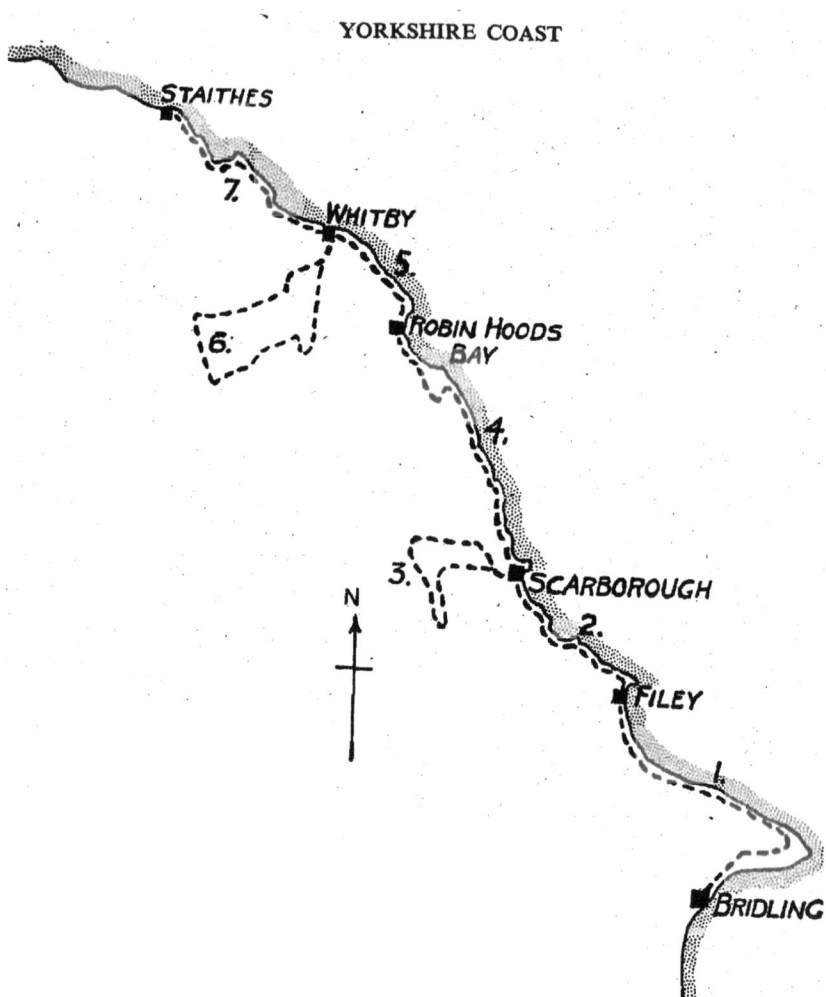

FIRST DAY

Bridlington has the usual amenities of a popular seaside resort. In the Old Town the Priory Church and the Bayle Gate (museum) are worth a visit. Take bus to Flamborough village. A ¼ mile before reaching village the road crosses the great ditch known as Danes Dyke, really a prehistoric fortification which cut off the headland from the rest of Yorkshire. Flamborough was known as "Little Denmark", and local dialect and customs still show traces of Danish descent. The road continues for a mile to Flamborough Head, with its old tower and lighthouse. Now take coastguard path going north past Selwicks Bay to North Landing, an inlet in the chalk cliffs from which a journey can be made by boat to the wonderful sea-caves hollowed out of the face of the cliffs. The path next passes Thornwick Bay, and then follow the Bempton, Buckton and Speeton Cliffs. These are some of the highest chalk cliffs in England, rising a sheer 400 feet from the sea, a gleaming white wall which continues for miles. It is best not to walk too close to the edge, as people have been blown over by the wind. In late May and June the interesting spectacle can be observed of the "egg-climbers" descending the cliffs by rope to collect the birds' eggs which lie on the rocky ledges. The eggs are used for food, and for dressing patent leather. Still following the coastline, you pass Reighton Sands to Primrose Valley and Muston Sands. It is less than a mile to FILEY, a small seaside resort. Half a mile to the north is the famous natural breakwater called Filey Brigg which can be explored at low tide.

Distance 14 miles.

SECOND DAY

From Filey follow sands or cliff-path to Carr Naze, with its view of the breakers dashing against Filey Brigg. The Naze was the site of a Roman signal station, and in rocky hollows amongst the cliffs are beautiful sea-pools. From Club Point there is another stretch of cliffs past Gristhorpe and Red

128   LET'S GO HIKING

Nab by Cayton Bay. Cayton Bay has a glorious stretch of sands and amateur geologists can hunt for fossils among the cliffs. It is worth climbing the cobbled lane from the waterworks to the main Scarborough-Filey road above, simply for the sake of the wonderful view of the bay and its wooded headlands. Continue north for a mile to a path or lane bearing right toward Cornelian Bay, so-called from the semi-precious stones which are found there. Various tracks lead through wooded dingles to the public gardens overlooking the South Bay of Scarborough.

SCARBOROUGH consists of the Old Town clustered beneath the ruined castle on the headland, and the newer streets of the holiday resort, stretching north and south. The castle was built shortly after the Norman conquest. Near it are the remains of a Roman signal station. Among the old houses facing the harbour is King Richard's House (housing a collection of relics). A grand walk is from the harbour round the Marine Drive beneath the cliffs of Castle Hill to Peasholm Glen (collection of rare plants and flowers). From there one can continue by path or miniature railway to the old smugglers' inn at Scalby Mills.

Distance 9 miles.

THIRD DAY

Close to Scarborough lies some of the most beautiful country in England. To-day's itinerary is intended to introduce you to it. First destination is Scalby village, which can be reached by bus from depot, or by walking north along Burniston Road and then taking first turning left past road bridge which now leads direct to Scalby. From here continue along road to Hackness. It is a stiff climb to the summit of Hay Brow—but worth it for the grand view over hills and sea. At Suffield turn left. Road presently descends into a delightful wooded, park-like landscape with tree-clad hills rising on either side. Two miles on and Hackness is reached. It is one of the prettiest villages in Yorkshire (interesting church). Hackness is the centre of a group of delightful little dales. Turn left with road and follow down beside the pools to cross-roads. Make for bridge across Derwent to Wrench Green, and from there follow path downstream by Cockrah Foot and Spiker's Hill to ruins of Ayton Castle. A ¼ mile away is Ayton village, on main Pickering-Scarborough road. Turn left for 100 yards where side-road will be seen bearing left. This leads through Forge Valley, a beautiful ravine with wooded hillsides rising almost sheer from the river. One and a half miles along is side-turning on right called Lady Edith's Drive. This leads you through Raincliffe Woods another 1½ miles to reedy Throxenby Mere. A short distance farther on you come to the main Scalby-Scarborough road, along which buses run to take you to SCARBOROUGH.

Distance 14 miles.

FOURTH DAY

Take a No. 113 bus to terminus by Burniston Road, and continue on over bridge (past Youth Hostel). A ¼ mile farther on right footpath will be seen leading across fields to cliff-top (*not* War Department road). From there coastguard-path runs north past Long Nab to Cloughton Wyke, a deep inlet ringed in by high cliffs. Proceed north by Rodger Trod to Hayburn Wyke, a deep-wooded glen through which a cascade runs down to the sea. Paths through the woods lead to the hotel at the top. From Red House an old road goes to Rigg Hall and then climbs steeply to War Dike (547 ft.), and the towering headland of Ravenscar. Ravenscar was once the seat of a development plan which failed. Now only grass-grown roads and isolated buildings remain. This is one of the highest points on the English coast, and grand views. Follow road uphill from hotel and turn right where lane leads to summit of High Moor (800 ft.). A mile farther on another lane bears right past railway to Stoupe Brow Cottage and the mouth of Stoupe Beck, from which point foreshore can be followed to ROBIN HOOD'S BAY. This is a quaint little fishing-port whose red-roofed houses are piled one above another along the single main street which drops to the harbour. It is a favourite artists' resort.

Distance 16 miles.

FIFTH DAY

This is a short day to allow exploration of Whitby. Take path to North Cheek; the headland overlooking the northern side of Robin Hood's Bay, where fine cliff scenery extends all the way to Whitby. Here and there waterfalls plunge over cliffs into sea. Go past Homerell Hole, White Stone Hole and Maw Wyke Hole to the lighthouse near Black Nab. Then comes Saltwick Bay and Saltwick Nab, where the East Cliff curves round to Whitby Abbey, standing four-square on its windswept hilltop. The abbey was originally founded by the Saxon St. Hilda in 657, though present structure dates only from 1220. Adjoining it is an interesting old church and a modern cross to Caedmon, the first English poet. A flight of steps leads down to the narrow streets of WHITBY. The local museum is interesting. There are also relics of Captain Cook who lived here and had his ships built in Whitby which were to take him round the world.

Distance 8 miles.

SIXTH DAY

To-day we forsake coast and follow the wooded valley of the Esk and its tributary, the Murk Esk. From Whitby take the road to Ruswarp and follow road alongside river through Glen Esk to Sleights. Beside the river here formerly stood the caravan belonging to " Romany " (well-known B.B.C. broadcaster). In the surrounding woods and fields he wandered with Raq in search of material for his talks. Cross river by railway station and follow main Whitby-Pickering road for nearly a mile to side-road leading along hillside for 3 miles to Grosmont, with its scanty remains of an old priory. Turn left again at Egton Bridge with its view of Arnecliffe Woods. Follow winding lane past Key Green, Randy Mere Reservoir and

THE YORKSHIRE COAST 131

Julian Park into valley of Wheeldale Beck. A mile or so upstream is the unique sight of a stretch of paved Roman road, It is known as Wade's Causeway, and has been excavated and left open for inspection. It connected the series of signal stations along the coast with the fortress at Malton, and along it when the signal fires blazed the Roman cavalry galloped to repel the Saxon invaders. Our route now crosses the beck and bears steeply to the left to the isolated village of Goathland in the wooded valley of the Murk Esk. In the neighbourhood are various waterfalls—Thomason Force, Mallyan Spout, and Nelly Ayre Force. From the railway station the road climbs to the summit of Sleights Moor (930 ft.), where it joins the main Whitby-Pickering road. Turn left and after $\frac{1}{4}$ mile turn right down winding lane leading into the deep-wooded glen of Little Beck. At hamlet of Little Beck (inn) a track leads upstream to Falling Foss, from where an old road leads to Red Gate on Whitby-Pickering road. Here a bus can be taken for last 4 miles to WHITBY.

Distance 14 miles.

SEVENTH DAY

Leave Whitby along the sea-shore, or at high tide by the road overlooking the sea. Upgang was an old smugglers' landing-place. A mile farther on take the steep road to Lythe Bank and the village of Lythe, overlooking the wooded valley in which stands Mulgrave Castle. Just before reaching village look for farm-road leading to Deepgrove Farm. Follow this. From the farm path follows well-wooded dell to Overdale Farm, and then follows airshafts marking line of railway tunnel to Cliff House. Beyond is the steep headland of Kettleness, overlooking beautiful Runswick Bay. Path descends from Kettleness towards Claymore Beck from which point the shoreline can be followed to Runswick village. Path along shore passes Lingrow Point and Rosedale Wyke to the "lost" harbour of Port Mulgrave. It was built to ship ironstone from the neighbouring mines, but the scheme was not a success, and the port now has a half-forgotten air. Path proceeds past Brackenberry Wyke to STAITHES, a small fishing-port that is even quainter than Robin Hood's Bay. The little town is crowded between sheer cliffs at the mouth of a small river, the houses being built in tiers into the rocky hillsides. At bottom of main street is the famous Cod and Lobster Inn. Captain Cook lived in a house by the quay while working at the local grocer's shop, before he ran away to Whitby to become a sailor. North of the town rises Boulby Cliff whose 666 feet make it the highest sea-cliff in England. From Staithes there are rail and bus services to Saltburn or south back to Whitby.

Distance, 12 miles.

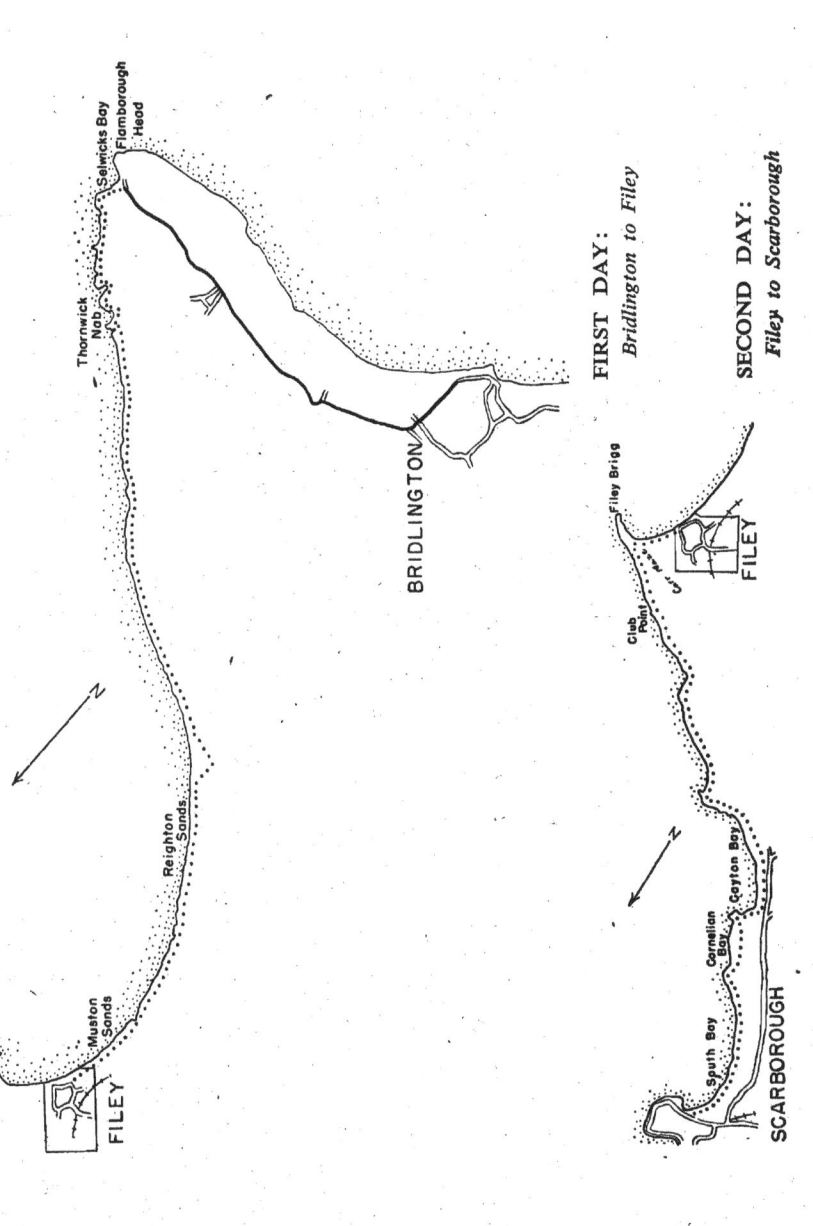

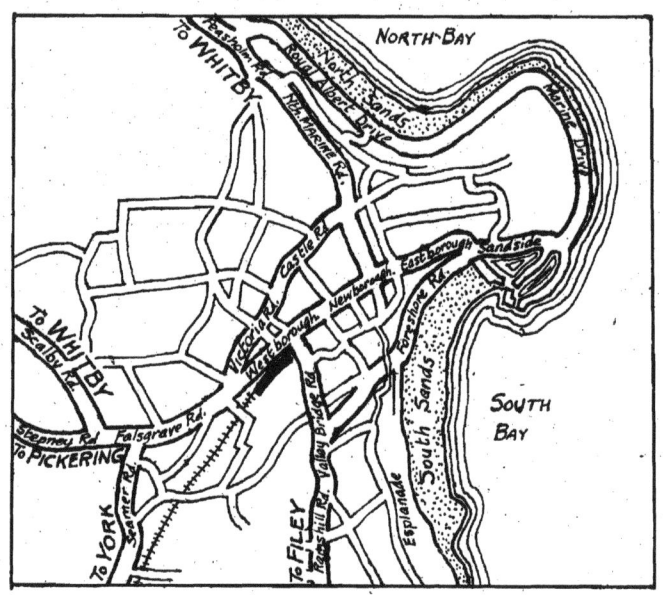

SCARBOROUGH

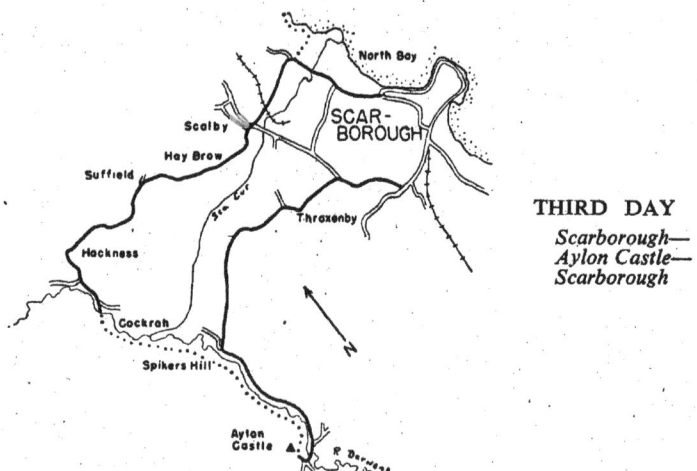

THIRD DAY

*Scarborough—
Aylon Castle—
Scarborough*

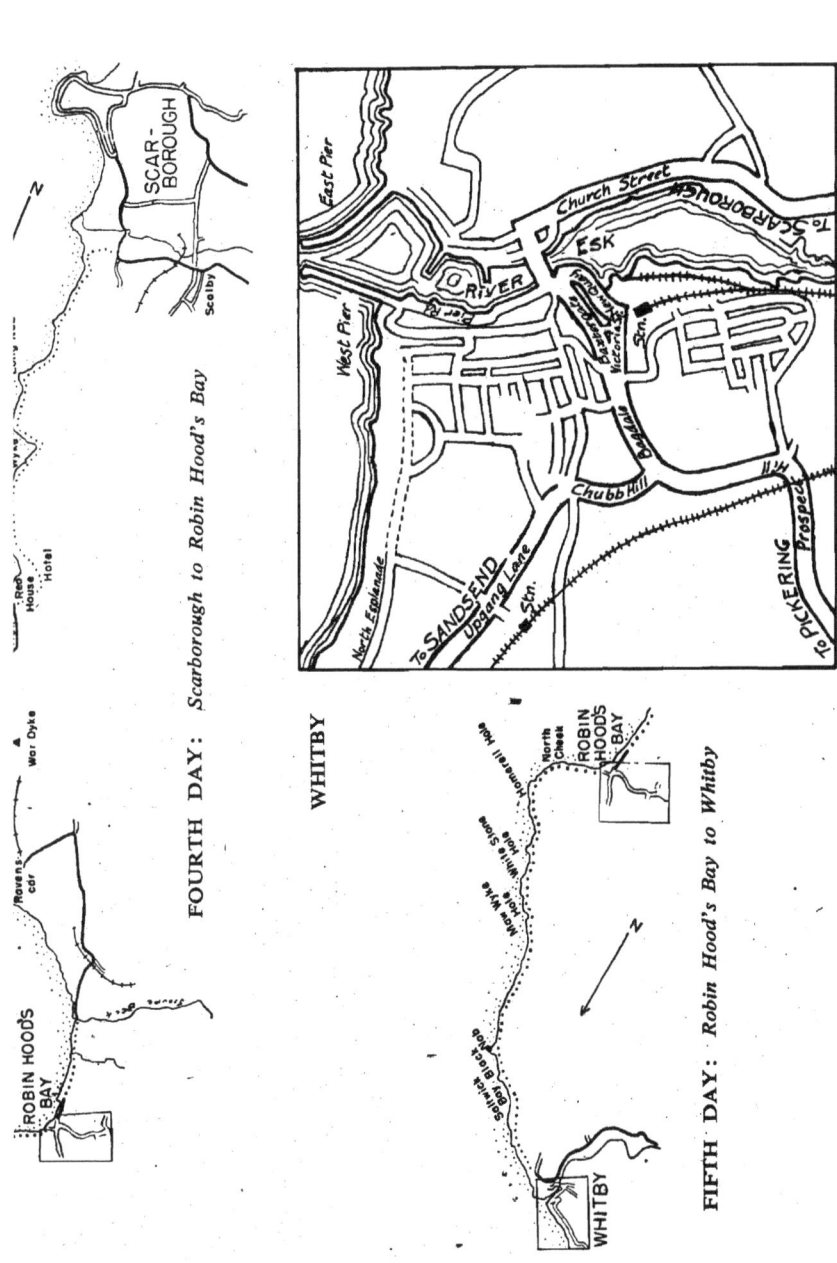

FOURTH DAY: *Scarborough to Robin Hood's Bay*

FIFTH DAY: *Robin Hood's Bay to Whitby*

SIXTH DAY: *Whitby—Egton Bridge—Sleights Moor—Whitby*

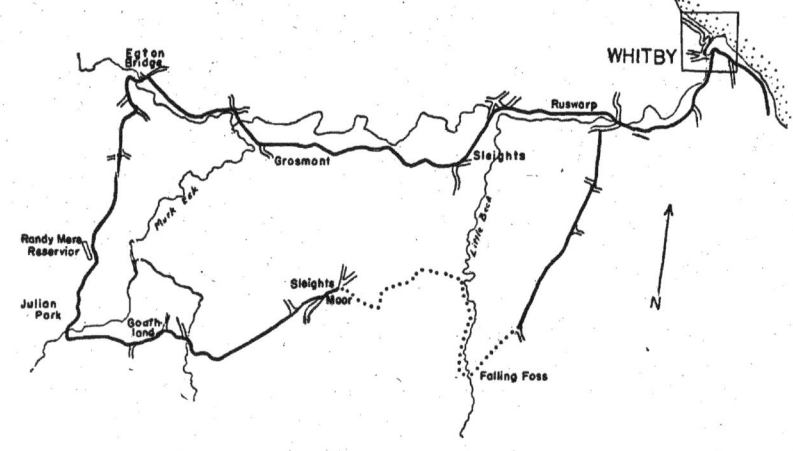

SEVENTH DAY: *Whitby to Staithes*

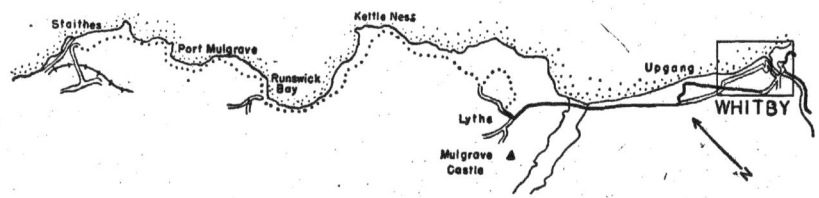

11. THE PEAK DISTRICT

High, heathery moorlands and deep, winding white-walled dales, green limestone uplands, whose springy turf makes the finest walking imaginable, lonely gritstone farmhouses and villages—these things stand out in my memory from tramping among the hills and valleys of the Peak. What area can include in such a small compass the sheer delight of Dovedale—surely one of the finest riverside walks in England? And then there is the grim grandeur of forbidden Kinder Scout. . . . The Peak is a district, not just a mountain. The name has been loosely given to the area known as Kinder Scout, because it is the highest point in this area. The Kinder Scout plateau is a block of elevated moorland, averaging slightly over 2,000 feet in height and covering several square miles. Another prominent feature of the landscape are the " edges ", where the moorland escarpments drop steeply to the valleys. The Peak District has two distinct types of scenery, the rough gritstone moorlands around Edale—arduous going this—and the rolling limestone grasslands with their steep, rock-walled valleys. It should be remembered that the term " Peak District " includes not only Derbyshire but considerable portions of Cheshire, Staffordshire and Yorkshire.

Summary of distances

1. BUXTON TO HOPE	15 miles
2. BAKEWELL	14 ,,
3. BUXTON	13 ,,
4. HARTINGDON	14 ,,
5. ASHBOURNE	15 ,,
6. HARTINGDON	15 ,,
7. BAKEWELL	14 ,,
Total Distance	100 ,,

Train travel
   Buxton and Bakewell. L.M.S.

Bus travel
   N.W. Road Car Co., Ltd.
   Sheffield Corporation Joint Services.
   Yorkshire Traction Co., Ltd.

Maps
   One-inch Ordnance Survey, sheets 45, 53.

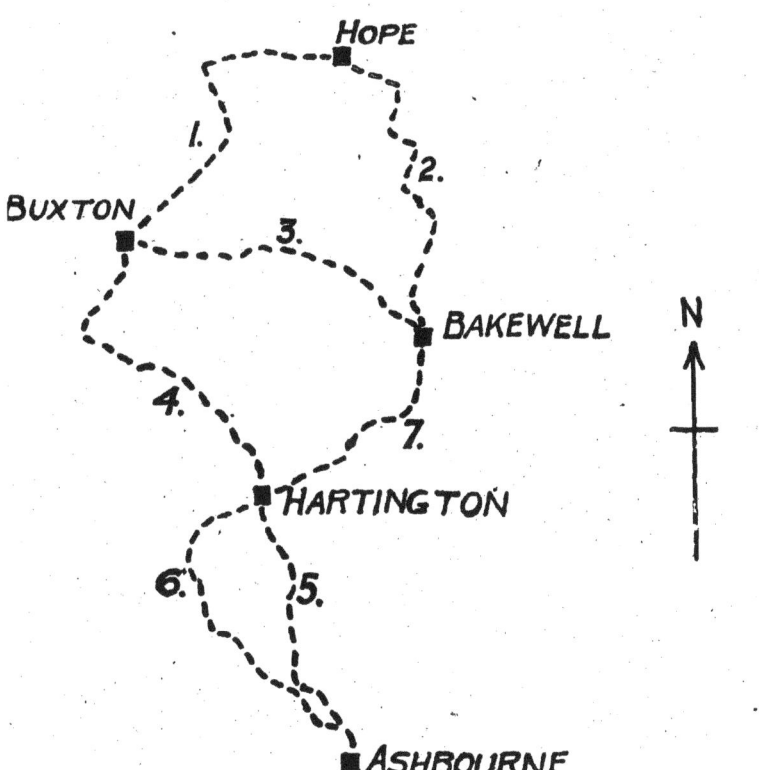

FIRST DAY

Buxton is a celebrated spa and one of the highest situated towns in England. Leave by the Chapel-en-le-Frith road to Fairfield (suggest bus), where an old road crosses golf-course to Water Swallows Green. At cross-roads in this village a path runs north-east to Upper End and then on $\frac{1}{2}$ mile to Peak Dale. Follow the road now to Smalldale, Laughman Tor, and Peak Forest. This was the centre of the ancient royal hunting-ground, and was formerly known as the " Gretna Green of the Peak " because of the many runaway marriages which took place here. Continue on to Old Dam, where road bears sharp left for $1\frac{1}{2}$ miles to Perryfoot. The summit on the light is Eldon Hill (1,543 ft.), one of the highest limestone hills. From its summit one can look over the green, turf-covered limestone uplands, criss-crossed with old prehistoric and Roman roads and old lead workings. This is delightful walking country in contrast to the rougher, heather-covered gritstone moors which begin only a mile to the north. In the side of Eldon Hill is Eldon Hole, a weird chasm 200 feet deep, once reputed to be bottomless. It has since been descended by explorers at various times. At Perryfoot continue past cross-roads for another mile to main Castleton–Chapel-en-le-Frith road. Turn right here. A few yards on take path left along summit of Rushup Edge—a grand ridge walk at 1,750 feet, looking down over the beautiful Vale of Edale and the heights of Kinder Scout. Highest point at 1,802 feet is marked by a prehistoric burial mound, known as the " Lord's Seat ". Path now descends steeply to Mam Nick, the pass through which the motor-road enters Edale. Descend to road, turn right to main highway, and $\frac{1}{4}$ mile farther on is old road, leading through the Winnats, a wild rock-walled gorge, leading to Castleton (old castle, caverns). Follow road to HOPE, $1\frac{1}{2}$ miles farther on.

Distance 15 miles.

SECOND DAY

Cross the bridge over Peakshole Water and follow path by river to Brough, site of the Roman fort, Anavio. Continue along the old road to Shatton, where you bear right along track curving Shatton Edge (1,367 ft). This moor contains various prehistoric stone circles, burial mounds, etc. Where track divides, bear left down to Abney. From here a track continues down Abney Clough to Stoke Ford. Follow upstream 1 mile to Nether Bretton through the winding vale of Bretton Clough. A $\frac{1}{4}$ mile on is Bretton (inn). Now take the turning for Eyam, once known as the " Plague village ". It contains various memorials of the Great Plague—the rocky dell called Cucklet Church, Mompesson's Well (in memory of a heroic vicar), old cottages, etc. Follow road south $\frac{1}{2}$ mile to junction with road through Middleton Dale. Near crossroads is a path leading south 3 miles over Longstone Moor to Great Longstone (inn). Follow road on to Rowdale House, where a track leads south over the hill to Holme Hall. Another $\frac{1}{4}$ mile brings you to BAKEWELL.

Distance 14 miles.

THIRD DAY

To-day's walk follows the Wye through a succession of wooded, rocky dales. Follow main Buxton road. After $\frac{1}{4}$ mile follow path on right upstream to old mill on outskirts of Ashford-on-the-Water—reputed to be the prettiest village in Derbyshire. Continue along Buxton road. Near ninth milestone a path turns right into Monsal Dale. This is a picturesque stretch where Wye curves round limestone crags of Fin Cop. At Little Longstone (inn) turn left along road to Cressbrook, and from there follow side-road leading along river to Millers Dale station. Path continues beside river through Chee Dale, where the sheer white cliffs of Chee Tor rise nearly 300 feet above you. Where cliffs rise sheer walkers have to make their way by stepping-stones placed in the river—quite an adventure! River continues through Wye

Dale under rocky slopes of Topley Pike and Pig Tor. Scenery, however, is spoilt in places by quarrying. At Pig Tor follow side-road on left up to Cowdale Farm, where a track runs along hillside for ¼ mile to rocks of "Lovers' Leap", overlooking the "Duke's Drive" which leads into BUXTON.

Distance 13 miles.

FOURTH DAY

From Buxton station proceed to western end of "Duke's Drive" and then follow road ¾ mile to Harpurhill. Here turn right. Half a mile on left is a lane leading by Countess Cliff and Diamond Hill to Turncliff Farm. Path continues over road to Leap Edge, crosses stream, and continues ¾ mile to main Buxton-Leek road, traversing Axe Bridge. This is the most southerly of the great gritstone hills, and reaches a height of 1,807 feet. It has been called the "Head of Rivers", for from its flanks flow five celebrated streams—the Goyt and Dane west to the Irish Sea, the Dove and Manifold south to join the Trent, and the Wye flowing east to join the Derwent. From Dove Head a path follows the infant river to Howe Green and Washgate and presently provides impressive views of Chrome Hill and Parkhouse Hill. Continue along the Dove some miles till you reach Crowdecote (inn). For the last 4 miles to Hartingdon the stream flows between high hillsides, crowned by the earthworks of Pilsbury Castle, an old British fortification. A ¼ mile below Moat Hall a path strikes left across the fields to HARTINGDON, a little, grey town grouped about a huge central square. Elizabethan Hartingdon Hall, now a Youth Hostel, boasts a room where Prince Charlie is reputed to have spent the night during his retreat from Derby in 1745.

Distance 14 miles.

FIFTH DAY

On this and the sixth day you go through two of the most lovely valleys in England—those of the Dove and the Manifold.

THE PEAK DISTRICT

Take the Warslow road. Three-quarters of a mile on left a path leads across fields to the River Dove. Where hills draw together about river is the entrance to the exquisite little Beresford Dale. Path continues downstream through Wolfacote Dale, more grassy and open. High up on right bank can be seen a cave where a tinker and his family once loved. At Lode Mill you strike a road. Follow this for ½ mile to Milldale, where the path continues downstream under the steep slopes of Raven's Tor. Here begins Dove Dale proper, described as the " fairest combination of wood, crag and river in England ". Much of it now is owned by the National Trust. The path passes the Dove Holes, two cavernous openings through which a subterranean river once flowed. Beyond lies the grandeur of Dove Dale—woods and cliffs, towering pinnacles of rock to which fanciful names have been given, such as " Lion Rock ", " Tissington Spires ", " Ilam Rock ", " Twelve Apostles ". Notice the curious natural arch beneath which the path climbs to Reynard's Cave. Presently path and river curve round between the peaks of Thorpe Cloud and Bunster Hill, which marks the end of the dale. The road which crosses the river goes west to Ilam with its Youth Hostel and east to Thorpe village, from which a road and path continue downstream to Mapleton, where a footpath leads over the ridge to ASHBOURNE. In Ashbourne the old inn where Boswell came with Dr. Johnson still survives. Ashbourne Hall is another place where Prince Charlie is reputed to have slept. He was proclaimed " King of England " in the market-place outside. Ashbourne Church is known as the " Cathedral of the Peak ".

Distance 15 miles.

SIXTH DAY

From Ashbourne take path over hill to Mapleton and follow river upstream to Thorpe and Ilam. This latter village is beautifully situated on a wooded reach of the Manifold known as " Paradise ". The River Manifold is almost as fascinating as the Dove; the two streams rise within ½ mile of each other and are never more than a mile or two apart. A footpath leads upstream from Ilam Hall (Youth Hostel) to Rushley Bridge, where an old lane turns left up a small side valley, and after 600 yards another old lane bears northwards across the fields along the Manifold to the ruins of Throwley Hall. In dry weather only the stony bed or " swallows " of the Manifold can be seen as the water follows an underground course until it emerges again in the grounds of Ilam Hall. The lane continues along the flank of Oldpark Hill to the ford at the junction of the Rivers Hamps and Manifold. This stream also has the habit of disappearing underground. From this point to Holme End, 6 miles north, the path follows the line of what was formerly the Manifold Light Railway. Opposite the ford is Beeston Tor, containing St. Bertram's Cave in which many prehistoric remains were found some years back. A mile higher upstream the black mouth of Thor's Cave can be seen gaping in the hillside 250 feet above the river. The view of Thor's Cave rising above the dark woodlands along the river is magnificent. Discoveries made here reveal that the cave was inhabited in Early British, Roman and Anglo-Saxon times. The path now winds continuously between hills which rise steeply to over 1,200 feet. At Warslow bridge continue along road past the mill to West Side and Hulme End (inn). From here it is a straight walk of $1\frac{1}{2}$ miles to HARTINGTON.

Distance 15 miles.

SEVENTH DAY

From Hartington follow main road $1\frac{1}{2}$ miles to Hartington station. A third of a mile farther on, at a bend in the road, the old road (shown as Green Lane on map) leads across main road to Midleton Common. We are now back in the typical wide-spreading limestone country, so different from the luxuriant dales of the Dove and the Manifold. Half a mile to the left of the track, near Gib Hill, is the stone circle called " Arbor Low ", and known as the " Stonehenge of the Midlands ". There are some forty stones, some up to 12 feet in length, lying inside a ditch and earthwork. Green Lane and its continuation Rake Lane lead you to Middleton-by-Youlgreave (inn). At cross-roads take path leading down Bradford Dale to Youlgreave (inn). At cross-roads take left-hand turn to Conkesbury Bridge, a mile away. This crosses the River Lathkill, which forms one of the loveliest dales in Derbyshire. Follow road on a mile to Newclose Farm. Here on right side of road a path brings you downhill towards BAKEWELL.

Distance 14 miles.

FIRST DAY: *Buxton to Hope*

SECOND DAY: *Hope to Bakewell*

THIRD DAY: Bakewell to Buxton

FOURTH DAY: Buxton to Hartington

FIFTH DAY: *Hartington to Ashbourne*

SIXTH DAY: *Ashbourne to Hartington*

SEVENTH DAY: *Hartington to Bakewell*

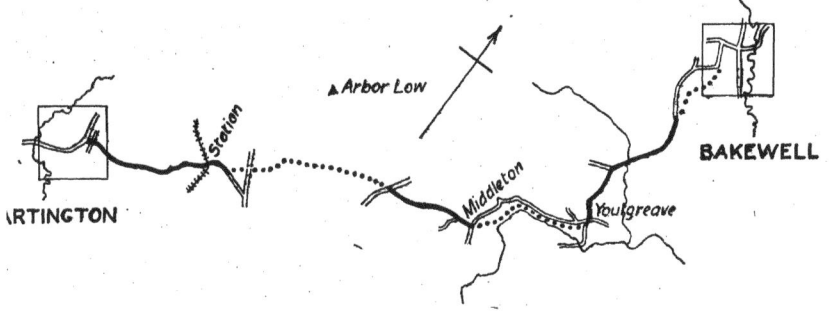

BUXTON

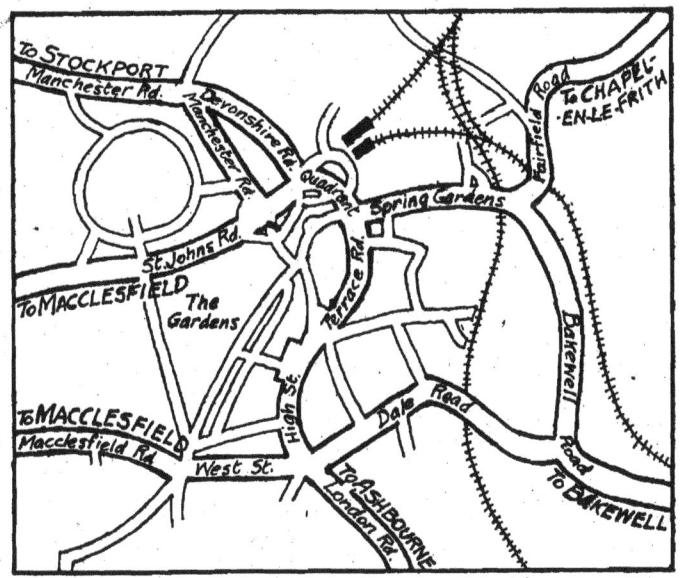

12. THE PILGRIMS' WAY

For 360 years during the Middle Ages The "Pilgrims' Way" from Winchester (which was a capital city longer than London has been) to Canterbury (which has ruled the religion of England for close on a thousand years) and the shrine of St. Thomas was trodden by millions of folk. For two centuries it was the most famed pilgrimage in Christendom. The old name still lives, and the memory of that famous pilgrimage of which Chaucer sang has not yet died out of the people's heart. It is still a pleasant thing to walk along it for the beauty of the country through which the old road runs, its historic associations and famous memories, the ancient churches and houses which lie on its course, will always attract those who love and reverence the past, and will lead many to follow in the footsteps of the medieval pilgrims along the Way to Canterbury.

Note.—The distance between Winchester and Canterbury by the " Pilgrims' Way " is at least 130 miles—too far, really, for a week's itinerary. The hiker has the choice, therefore, either of covering certain sections of the route by bus or by covering the Guildford-Canterbury section. Anyone who can spare 10-11 days can cover the whole distance. Again, weekenders around London may want to cover the road in two or more periods. This can easily be done, although accommodation then is often a problem to be faced.

Summary of distances

1. WINCHESTER (ST. CROSS) TO NEW ALRESFORD   10 miles
2. ALTON . . . . . 11 ,,
3. FARNHAM . . . . . 10 ,,
4. SHALFORD (GUILDFORD) . . . 12 ,,
5. DORKING . . . . . 12 ,,
6. MERSTHAM (REDHILL) . . . 10 ,,
7. WESTERHAM . . . . 13 ,,
8. WROTHAM . . . . . 13 ,,

THE PILGRIMS' WAY

Summary of distances (contd.)
9. DETLING (MAIDSTONE)	. . . . .	15 miles
10. CHARING	. . . . . .	12 ,,
11. CANTERBURY	. . . . . .	18 ,,
Total Distance	. . . . .	136 ,,

Train travel
Winchester and Canterbury. S.R.

Bus travel
Aldershot and District Traction Company, Ltd.
London Transport.
Maidstone and District Motor Services, Ltd.
East Kent Road Car Company, Ltd.

Maps
One-inch Ordnance Survey, sheets 168, 169, 170, 171, 172, 173 (N.P.).

THE PILGRIMS' WAY

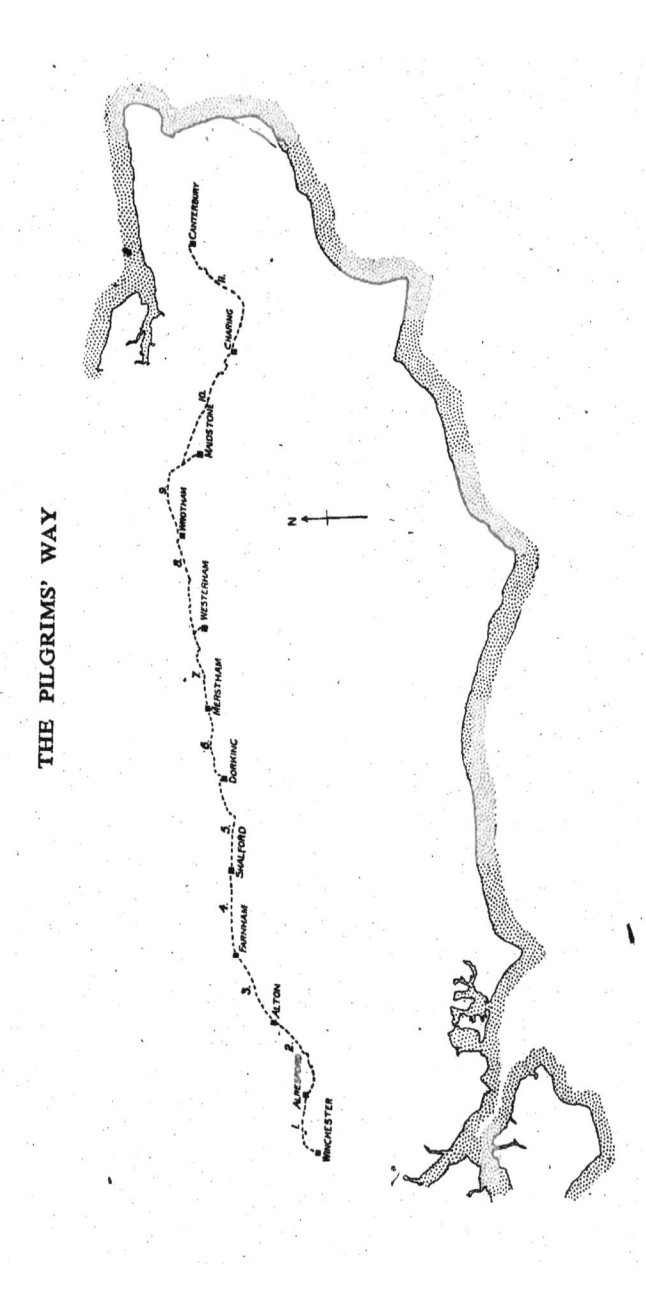

FIRST DAY

The true pilgrim will wish to start on his modern pilgrimage from the Hospital of St. Cross, 1½ miles west of Winchester. It was here that the medieval pilgrims gathered on the first night prior to setting out for Canterbury. It is a lovely place, full of interest, and the "Wayfarer's Dole" (a horn of ale and bread) is still issued to those who call. Fortified with this refreshment, the way leads along the banks of the Itchen to Winchester (maginficent cathedral, college, Godbegot House, Jane Austen's house, etc.) and by way of Jewry Street into Hyde Street. Turn right at St. Bartholomew's Church, then left along Caxton Street, at the end of which the "Nuns' Walk" starts. This takes you along the side of the Itchen to the church at Kings Worthy. Opposite the lych-gate is the post-office. Turn down a lane to the right of post-office which brings you back to the Itchen. Follow along its banks past Martyrs Worthy and Chilland, coming out at Itchen Abbas Church. Here turn sharp right along the road crossing the river, and then first left and proceed through Avington Park. Arriving at the hamlet of Ovington (inn), turn left for a short distance, then, just before reaching the river, turn right, cross the main road, bearing left until you reach an inn. Near-by is the Tichborne estate (famous for its "Dole" and a notorious lawsuit). The original "Pilgrims' Way" proceeds straight ahead to Bishops Sutton, but you will turn left for New Arlesford ("New" is rather a misnomer, for it is an ancient, pleasant town).

Distance 10 miles.

SECOND DAY

To regain the "Pilgrims' Way" follow the main Alton road to Bishops Sutton, where once stood a bishop's palace. From here on to the next village of Ropley Dean the Way follows the main road. At the far end of Ropley Dean stands the Chequers Inn. Here the old track branched off to the right, running more or less parallel with the present main road. It is difficult to follow, but in order to get off the main road turn right along a road to Gilbert Street, then left for ½ mile to cross-roads, and right. Two and a half miles farther on lies Four Marks, where you once more come to the main road. As heavy motor traffic dashes past you along this road you may decide to take bus to Alton, passing through the village of Chawtor, where Jane Austen lived and where she wrote some of her greatest works. A road to the right, signposted " Selborne ", may well tempt you to visit this historic and lovely spot, the home of Gilbert White.

Distance 11 miles.

THIRD DAY

From Alton to Farnham the old road followed the present main road. As there is little attraction for any walker to follow a main road, I suggest either covering this distance by bus, or else walking alongside the River Way which runs parallel. It is not an easy journey, but a pleasant one. It is worth while mentioning here that the Way had certain definite characteristics or " habits " in its planning, and these are explained in detail by Hilaire Belloc in his book *The Old Road*. FARNHAM was a place of capital importance in the old days.

Distance 10 miles.

FOURTH DAY

From Farnham take bus along the main Guildford road for 3 miles as far as Whitewaysend. Here you descend and branch off right for Seale, leaving the Hog's Back on your left. Seale has an interesting church, beautifully situated. Your way lies through a quiet road with almost no traffic on it. Passing the hamlet of Shoelands (taking its name from " School "—to beg), you arrive at Puttenham (inn). Immediately opposite the Jolly Farmers Inn you take a path, leading across Puttenham Heath. Here in 1851 Queen Victoria held a great review

THE PILGRIMS' WAY 155

of troops: it is now a golf-course. It is 1½ miles until you strike the main Godalming road. Compton (an interesting church and a pleasant village) lies on your right. You pass near Limnerslease (the painter Watts's home and an art gallery) and then through a wooden gate enter Monkshatch Park. You follow the path through this park and carry on until you arrive at Sandy Lane. This brings you out on the main Godalming road and to the River Wey. GUILDFORD lies ¾ mile on your left, and can be reached by bus.
Distance 12 miles.

FIFTH DAY

Return along the Shalford road until you reach the foot of St. Catherine's Church. Follow a road which takes you to the north-west corner of Chantries Wood. A track now takes you on to St. Martha's Church and then along the northern side of Weston Wood and down to the main Albury-Shere road, which you cross by the somewhat imposing Catholic Apostolic Church. Going through Albury Park you will notice a remarkable yew hedge. Bear to right, cross the stream, and then along a fine avenue of lime trees, past some picturesque cottages and into Shere (inn). South of the church a path takes you to Gomshall, where you cross the main road, taking a road, first on your left, due north until you reach a guide-post marked " Blindoak Gate ". Here you turn right and proceed through Oaken Grove, traversing Ranmore Common and passing Denbies. This brings you out near the Dorking Lime Works. A bus will take you down to DORKING (a rather difficult place for accommodation at week-ends).
Distance 12 miles.

SIXTH DAY

From Dorking proceed north on the London road beyond the cemetery; then turn off right, passing Castle Mill, to reach that famed beauty spot, Box Hill, now the property of the

National Trust. Remember that the old pilgrims nearly always followed the southern slope of the hills where the soil was driest. You will do the same, and the road presents little difficulty and much freedom of choice. All the day the vista is really grand. Your path continues to Brockham Warren. Near the bottom of the wood there is a gap in the hedge. It leads you into a fine avenue of ancient yews. (The yew trees are to be found frequently along the Way.) This leads to the chalk-pits. Next you traverse Pepple Coombe, and from there follow near the ridges of Buckland Hills, the summit of Colley Hill and Reigate Hill. You cross the London road now, taking the second road right a little way up. This takes you along the top of Gatton Park, where there is a Grecian Town Hall, a small open-to-the-air building. It has a notorious history, for here two members were elected for Parliament to represent this constituency with practically no voters. Merstham is now reached, and as it lies on the main Brighton road you will be well advised to take bus or train into REDHILL for the night.

Distance 10 miles.

SEVENTH DAY

Return to Merstham. At the top end of the village you will see a road turning right. It leads past a number of small residences. Half a mile along it there is a path leading off left in a north-easterly direction. This brings you uphill to the top of the ridge, known as the White Hill and looking down over Quarry Hangers. (The road below Quarry Hangers is a pleasant walk also.) The ridge track brings you out near a cross-roads, near which stands an ancient tower. On your right is Arthur's Seat, a spur on which there once was a prehistoric camp. Follow the road east with wonderful views over the country south, culminating at a spot known as " The View ", a popular pleasure-spot at the week-end. A path at the south-east corner of " The View " takes you down to the pleasant village of Godstone. Otherwise follow on and over the Caterham Road, past Marden Castle until you strike a steep hill

THE PILGRIMS' WAY 157

just above Flinthall Farm. It is a good mile, but with fine views often on your right, to a cross-roads. Turn right and follow the ridge road until you reach a main cross-roads. The road to your right leads steeply down to Titsey, where by the church you turn left and follow a road over an open part of the country until you reach a main road. Cross this and follow on south of Hill Park until you strike the main London road from Westerham. Turn right and you arrive at WESTERHAM (the birthplace of General Wolfe).

Distance 13 miles.

EIGHTH DAY

Return to the place where you joined the main London road yesterday and then turn right by a road which brings you to the boundary of Chevening Park. The old Way ran straight through this park, but you should turn left for $\frac{1}{4}$ mile when you find a public footpath right that takes you through a wood and Chevening Park, emerging close to the mansion and Chevening Church. South of the churchyard is a track leading east. Half a mile on it brings you to a road and to a main road. Here turn left and then first right. The signpost shows Otford and West Pilgrims' Way. Otford is a delightful village with a famous history. Despite its rustic appearance Otford is only 20 miles from London, and can be reached by fast train in just over half an hour. From Otford the Way follows right just beyond the railway station, and then on straight for several miles. You keep due east all the time, ignoring all roads to right or left. When you reach a large fruit orchard take a forward track which brings you out close to WROTHAM.

Distance, 13 miles.

NINTH DAY

Go north to the main road. Here you see a large modern roadside café, ineptly named " Ye Old Pilgrims' Tea Rooms ".

Just at its back a road turns right. In time it turns into a mere track, but there is no difficulty in following it. Half a mile beyond Bunker's Farm you come out on a road, turn right and follow it right down to Paddlesworth and Snodland. There can be few more unpleasant towns in southern England. Its main industry is cement manufacture, but I could not even find a café, Proceed to the ancient church, and just south of it a path leads down to the ferry-boat (fare 2d.—the ferry closes between 2-4 p.m.). It is only 50 yards wide here across the Medway. On the other side you find yourself on a desolate marsh. The right-hand raised path leads you to a ruined church and ¾ mile farther on is Burham, another depressing spot. Turn right and follow straight on for nearly 2 miles until you strike another road. Cross this and follow a path that brings you out on the main Maidstone road. Immediately opposite is another path that follows round below the ridge until you strike a road again taking you into Boxley. At the top of the village a country road leads you on to DETLING. As you are unlikely to get accommodation here, a bus will take you into Maidstone.

Distance 15 miles.

TENTH DAY

From Detling to Charing your road runs almost straight without difficulty. Although the railway and the main road lie not far on your right, you find yourself in a countryside which is peaceful and unchanged, the only sign of modernity being the tractor. All the day you have fine views over the Weald of Kent. You pass through quiet villages such as Thurnham and Hollingbourne, but often for miles you have the countryside to yourself. You pass Lenham Sanatorium, reputed to be the coldest spot in England during the winter. A mile beyond you come to Cobham Farm, and here you find the Way has been enclosed. Perhaps you can find a cross-country track, otherwise you must return to the main road on your right, follow it for a mile, then turn left and right,

THE PILGRIMS' WAY

and this brings you out north of CHARING, another historic spot.

Distance 12 miles.

ELEVENTH DAY

Your route to-day deviates far from the present more direct main road to Canterbury, but the gain is yours. From Charing you walk up to the main Canterbury road and along it for 200 yards. Now turn right, which leads on to Burnt House. Here you strike a path along the foot of Longbeach Wood that brings you to Dunn Street. Crossing the road here, another path leads you to Eastwell Park. During the war there were several military camps here, and it is rather difficult to detail which path to take. There are so many. Your objective, however, is Boughton Lees (inn) where you cross a main road and strike north-easterly for Soakham Downs. The old Way is rather confusing now, but you will strike through King's Wood to Godmersham Church. Follow the road left of the church to Godmersham Park (the mansion). Note: an alternative is to omit Godmersham from Soakham Downs and follow farther north along the edge of King's Wood and Godmersham Park until you strike a track leading east towards Hurst Farm. If, however, you have reached Godmersham Park Mansion, cross the east side of the park, close to the small river, until you reach a gate at the corner. The other side a small path leads you alongside the fence, past a hopfield on your right, and this brings you out on a road leading through Mountain Street into the lovely village of Chilham. (The Way used to run through the grounds of Chilham Castle, but these are now enclosed.) From Chilham (inn) you proceed to the main road, but immediately across the road you follow north to the quaintly-named village of Old Wives' Lees (a pilgrims' deviation for some reason or other). You turn right again and return to the main Canterbury road, which you now follow 1½ miles to the Chartham cross-roads. Turn left for Chartham Hatch and then right through delightful woods to

Bigbury Camp and on to Harbledown. Here is the old leper-house of St. Nicholas, now an alms-house (well worth a visit). A short distance on you reach the top of Harbledown Hill, and here you get, like the pilgrims of old, your first sight of the Cathedral. Your goal is almost reached. A mile on is the Westgate, reached, alas, through a somewhat incongruous collection of buildings and houses. But when you stand at the " Martyrdom " in the Cathedral, you will feel, perhaps, some of the thrill the old pilgrims must have felt at this very same spot.

Distance 18 miles.

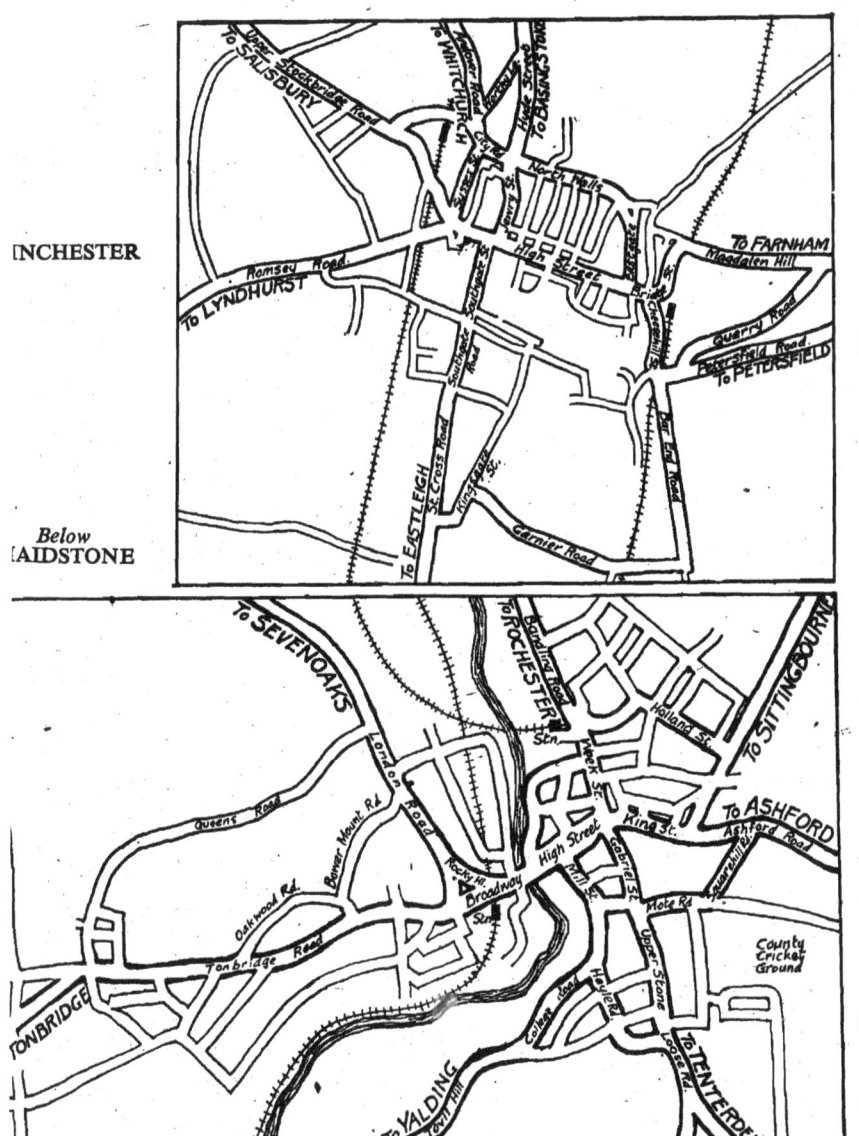

FIRST DAY: *Winchester to New Alresford*

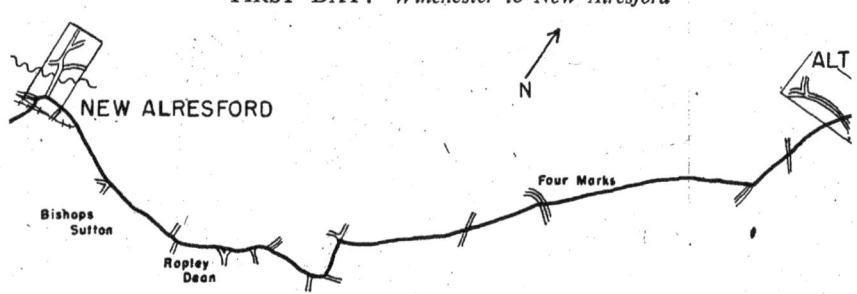

SECOND DAY: *New Alresford to Alton*

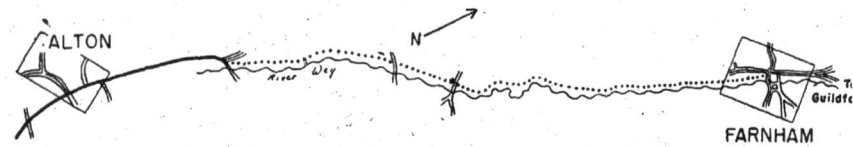

THIRD DAY: *Above*   FOURTH DAY: *Below*

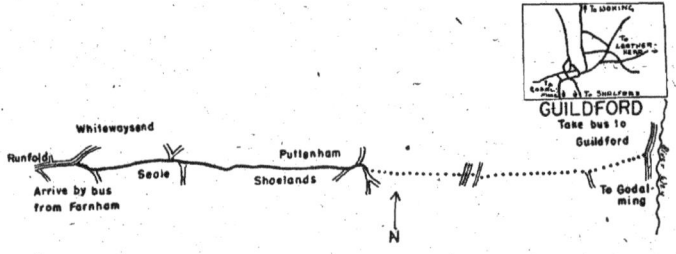

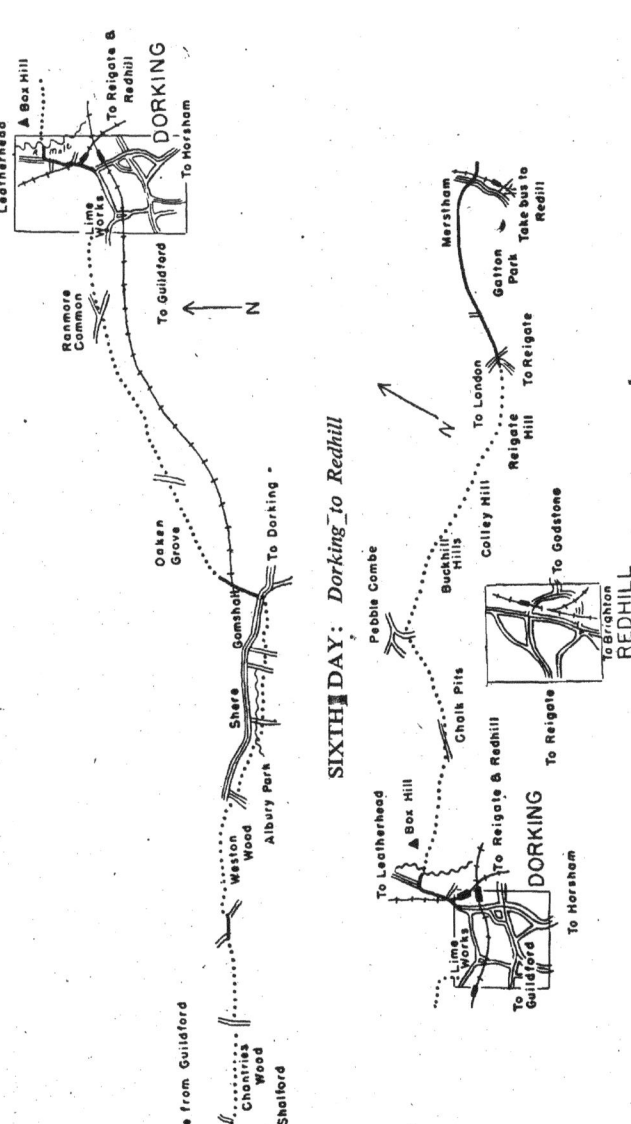

FIFTH DAY: *Guildford to Dorking*

SIXTH DAY: *Dorking to Redhill*

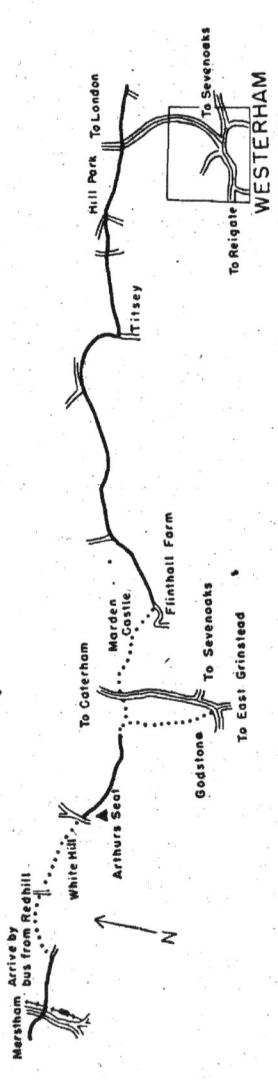

SEVENTH DAY: *Redhill to Westerham*

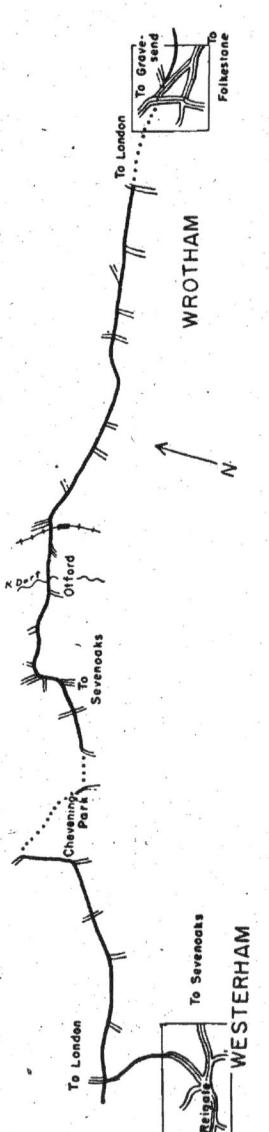

EIGHTH DAY: *Westerham to Wrotham*

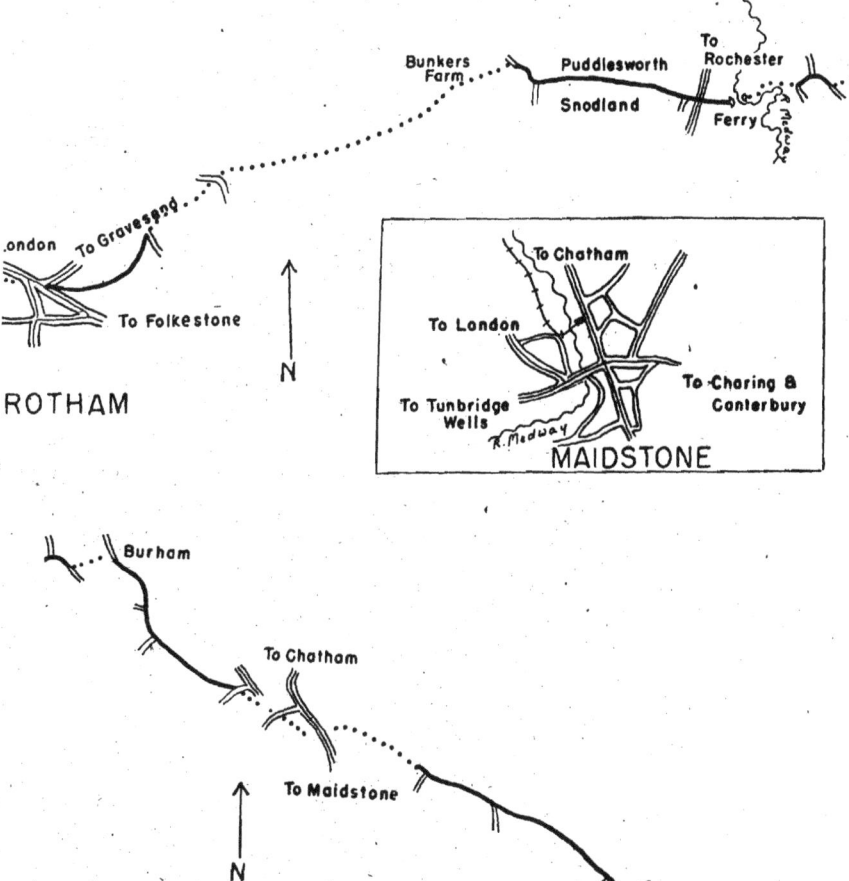

NINTH DAY: *Wrotham to Detling*

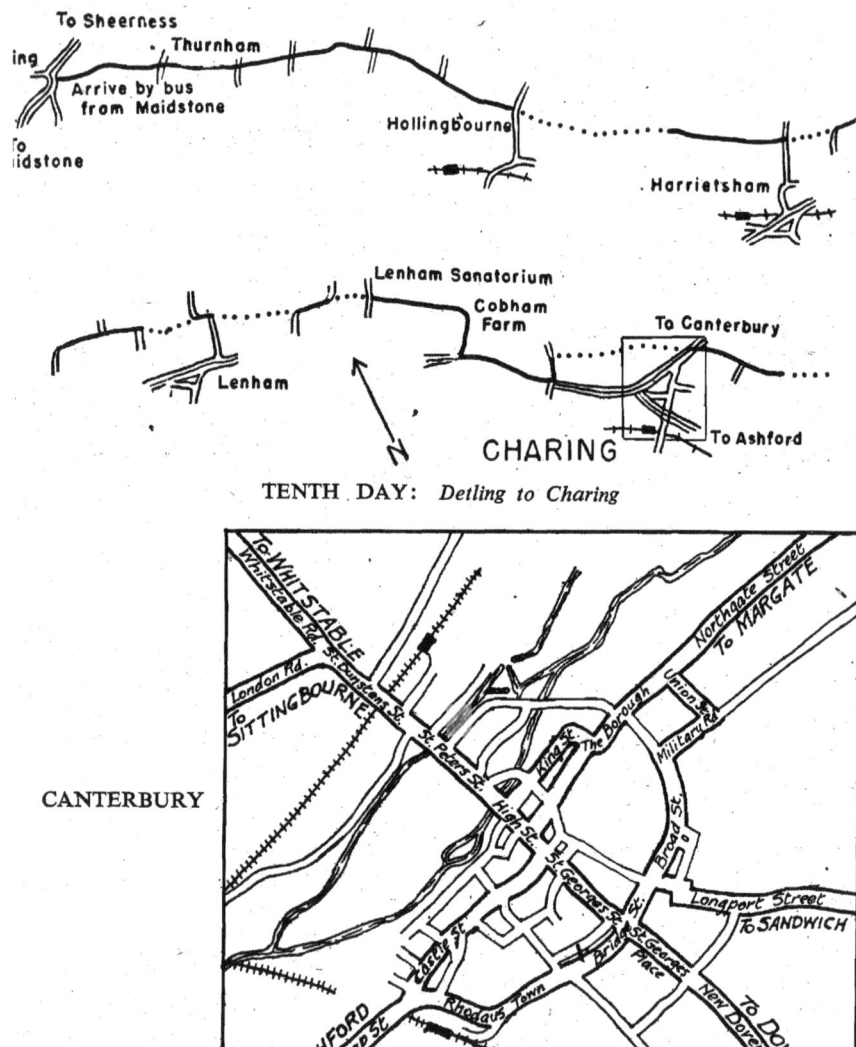

TENTH DAY: *Detling to Charing*

CANTERBURY

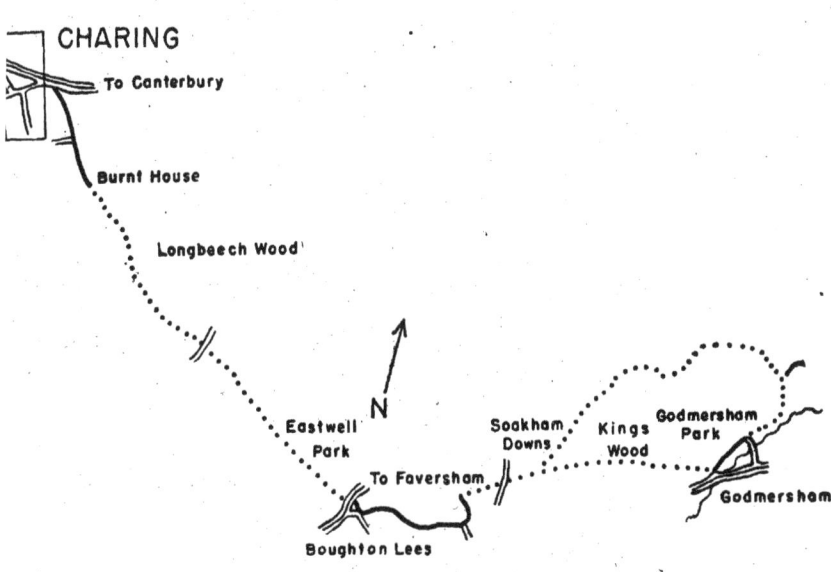
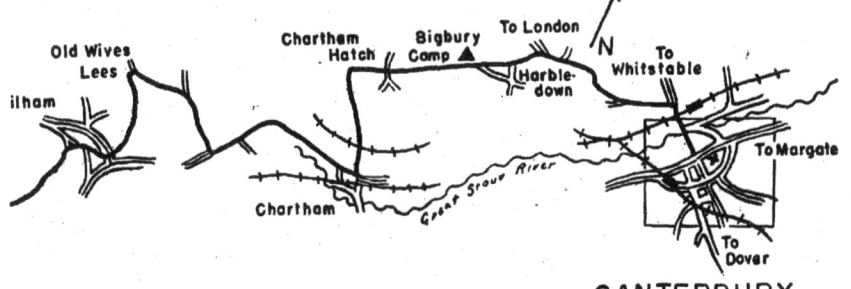

ELEVENTH DAY: *Charing to Canterbury*

APPENDIX A

USEFUL ADDRESSES

Ramblers' Association, 20 Buckingham Street, London, W.C.2.

National organizations providing holidays of a type suitable for walkers :

The Holiday Fellowship Ltd., 142 Great North Way, London, N.W.4.

The Co-operative Holidays Association, Birch Heys, Cromwell Range, Fallowfield, Manchester.

The Workers' Travel Association, 49 Cannon Street, London, E.C.4.
(*The above do not provide casual overnight accommodation.*)

Youth Hostels Association, Howard's Gate, Meadow Green, Welwyn Garden City, Herts.

For information about camping :
The Camping Club, 38 Grosvenor Gardens, London, S.W.1.

Helpful for the hiker-cyclist is :
The Cyclists' Touring Club, 3 Craven Hill, London, W.2.

Local Chambers of Commerce and Information Bureaux in many towns have lists of accommodation available.

Ordnance Survey maps :
Edward Stanford, Ltd., 12 Long Acre, London, W.C.2.
(If unobtainable locally), or in the event of difficulty:
Director General, Ordnance Survey, Chessington, Surrey.

The Best Emergency Ration —
to keep you going

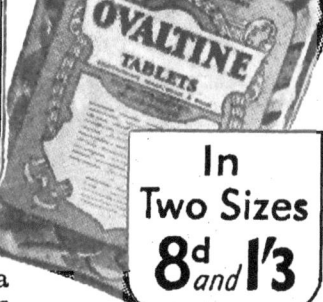

In Two Sizes 8^d and 1/3

NEVER go hiking without a supply of 'Ovaltine' Tablets for eating. They provide 100 per cent. concentrated nourishment in a convenient and delicious form.

'Ovaltine' Tablets possess the pre-eminent restorative and revitalising properties of 'Ovaltine' and will help to sustain strength and stamina over prolonged periods. They are invaluable during a long walk or in an emergency. Remember that 'Ovaltine' Tablets are the most satisfying emergency ration available. They are obtainable in two handy sizes for the pocket.

OVALTINE Tablets
for Sustenance and Stamina

170   LET'S GO HIKING

Motor-bus timetables (when available) can be obtained from the addresses given below. In writing enclose 6d., and state the area for which the timetable is wanted, as some companies issue several portions for the districts covered by them:

1. **Stratford on Avon**

    Midland Red Motor Omnibus Co., Ltd., Bearwood, Birmingham.
    Stratford Blue Motor Services, Bearwood, Birmingham.

2. **Cotswolds**

    Midland Red Motor Omnibus Co., Ltd., Bearwood, Birmingham.
    Bristol Tramways, Bristol.
    City of Oxford Motor Services, Oxford.

3. **North Wales**

    Crossville Motor Services, Ltd., Chester.

4. **Dorset**

    Wilts and Dorset Motor Services, Ltd., Salisbury.
    Southern National Omnibus Co., Ltd., Exeter.
    Western National Omnibus Co., Ltd., Exeter.

5. **Wye Valley**

    Bristol Tramways, Bristol.
    Red and White Services, Ltd., Chepstow, Mon.
    Western Welsh Omnibus Co., Ltd., Cardiff.

6. **Pembrokeshire**

    Western Welsh Omnibus Co., Ltd., Cardiff.

7. **Lizard**

    Western National Omnibus Co., Ltd., Exeter.

Let's go HIKING
in comfort

...in the special comfort of a Clarks walking shoe, its supple leather chosen to stand up to the wear and tear of country bypaths, and only a hint of its sturdiness to be guessed from its trim lines.

Clarks Shoes

Sold by leading retailers in nearly every town
C. AND J. CLARK LTD. (WHOLESALE ONLY) STREET, SOMERSET

8. Dunkery to Tintagel
Western National Omnibus Co., Ltd., Exeter.
Southern National Omnibus Co., Ltd., Exeter.

9. English Lakeland
Ribble Motor Services, Ltd., Preston.
Cumberland Motor Services, Whitehaven.

10. Yorkshire Coast
East Yorkshire Motor Services, Ltd., Hull.

11. Peak District.
Sheffield Corporation Joint Services, Sheffield.
Yorkshire Traction Co., Ltd., Barnsley.
N.W. Road Car Co., Ltd., Charles Street, Stockport.

12. Winchester to Canterbury
Aldershot and District Traction Co., Ltd., Aldershot.
London Transport, 55 Broadway, London, S.W.1.
Maidstone and District Motor Services, Ltd., Maidstone.
East Kent Road Car Co., Ltd., Harbledown, Canterbury.

Hiking is incomplete without a good Rucsack

The B.B. ALPINE fulfils all requirements of lightness, comfort and capacity

**Order from your dealer now
15" for ladies.   17" for men**

→ This name is your safeguard of dependability

MADE ONLY BY
BROWN BEST & CO.
44 TARN STREET, S.E.1

(Wholesale Only)

The best in a day's walk

Tudor Cottages, Chiddingstone, Kent.

NUGGET
BOOT POLISH

IN BLACK, BROWN & DARK BROWN

Supreme for Quality

Burlington Lane, London, W.4

N/NF

APPENDIX B

A FEW BOOKS TO READ

THIS list has been carefully prepared in the hope that it may be of use to hikers. No attempt is made to give a list of all the books dealing with the areas of country through which the itineraries pass. My aim is to give the titles of a few books on each walk which can help you appreciate your surroundings better. Some of the books named are at present out of print, but it is often possible to consult them in your local public library.

GENERAL SERIES

Highways and Byways (Macmillan)
Little Guides (Methuen)
King's England (Hodder and Stoughton)
Wayfarer (Methuen)
British Heritage (Batsford)
Face of Britain (Batsford)
Pilgrims' Library (Batsford)
Methuen's Companion Books
Ward Lock's Guide Books
Blue Guides (Murray)
Dunlop Guides
Michelin Guides
Shell Guides
Penguin Guides
Historical Monuments Commission Reports

GENERAL BOOKS

How to See England, by E. Vale (Methuen)
Camping and Hiking for All, by W. Holt-Jackson (Routledge)
Face of the Home Counties, by H. Clunn (Simpkin Marshall)

176 LET'S GO HIKING

1. The Shakespeare Country

Rambles in Shakespeare's Country, by J. H. Wade (Methuen)
Summer Days in Shakespeare's Land, by C. G. Harper (Chapman & Hall)
Things Seen in Shakespeare's Country, by Clive Holland (Seeley, Service)
The Avon and Shakespeare's Country, by A. G. Bradley (Methuen)
The Old Houses of Stratford, by H. E. Forrest (Methuen)
Shakespeare's Homeland, by W. S. Brassington (Dent)
In Shakespeare's Warwickshire, by O. Baker (Simpkin Marshall)

2. The Cotswolds

Cotswold Country, by H. J. Massingham (Batsford)
The Cotswolds, by J. Moore (Chapman & Hall)
A Cotswold Book, by H. W. Timperly (Cape)
Footpath Way in Gloucestershire, by A. Gissing (Dent)
A Cotswold Village, by J. A. Gibbs (Cape)
Wold without End, by H. J. Massingham (Sanderson)

3. North Wales

In Praise of Wales, by A. G. Bradley (Methuen)
Tramping through Wales, by J. C. Moore (Dent)
On Foot in North Wales, by P. Monkhouse (Maclehose)
Things Seen in North Wales, by W. T. Palmer (Seeley, Service)
The Romance of Wales, by A. G. Bradley (Methuen)
A Wayfarer in Wales, by Watkin Davies (Methuen)
Wild Wales, by George Borrow (new cheap edition by Collins)
Welsh Border Country, by G. Jones (Batsford)
In the March and Borderland of Wales, by A. G. Bradley (Methuen)

4. Unspoilt Dorset

Companion into Dorset, by D. Gardiner (Methuen)
Thomas Hardy's Wessex, by H. Lee (Macmillan)
Rambles in Dorset, by J. H. Wade (Methuen)

178   LET'S GO HIKING

The Hardy Country, by C. G. Harper (Chapman & Hall)
The Marches of Wessex, by Harvey Darton (Newnes)

5. The Wye Valley

The Book of the Wye, by E. Hutton (Methuen)
Coming Down the Wye, by R. Gibbings (Dent)
Hereford and Tintern, by G. Foord

6. The Pembrokeshire Coast

A Wayfarer in Wales, by W. Watkin Davies (Methuen)
The Romance of Wales, by A. G. Bradley (Methuen)
History of Little England beyond Wales, by E. Laws
Description of Pembrokeshire, by G. Owen

7. Round the Lizard Peninsula

The South Cornish Coast, by W. Watkin Davies (Methuen)
The Cornwall Coast, by Arthur Salmon
Unknown Cornwall, by C. Simpson (Lane)
Cornish Coasts and Moors, by Folliott-Stokes (Stanley Paul)
Walking in Cornwall, by J. R. A. Hockin (Methuen)

8. Dunkery to Tintagel

North Devon Coast, by C. G. Harper (Unwin)
North Cornwall Coast, by C. G. Harper (Unwin)
The Cornwall Coast, by Arthur Salmon
Rambles in Devon, by J. H. Wade (Methuen)

9. English Lakeland

The English Lakes, by W. T. Palmer (Black)
Walking in the Lake District, by H. H. Symonds (Maclehose)
Wild Lakeland, by M. MacBride (Black)
Companion into Lakeland, by Maxwell Fraser (Methuen)
Things Seen in the English Lakes, by W. T. Palmer (Seeley, Service)
Days in Lakeland, by E. M. Ward (Methuen)
  Various books by George Abraham (Methuen)

Every Slice is Always Nice

Hovis is more than just a delicious bread: it is a food in itself. Dainty, golden-brown Hovis makes every meal more appetising and nutritious.

Best Bakers Bake it

Macclesfield

Walk on Leather for Health

Issued by The United Tanners' Federation

E.W.G.

APPENDICES

10. Yorkshire Coast

Striding Through Yorkshire, by A. J. Brown (Country Life)
The Romance of the Yorkshire Coast, by H. L. Gee (Methuen)
A Book of Yorkshire, by J. H. Fletcher (Methuen)

11. The Peak District

On Foot in the Peak, by P. J. Monkhouse (Maclehose)
Tramping in Derbyshire, by W. T. Palmer (Country Life)
High Peak to Sherwood, by T. L. Tudor (Robert Scott)

12. Pilgrims' Way

The Old Road, by Hilaire Belloc (Constable)
The Pilgrims' Way, by J. Cartwright (Murray)
The Canterbury Pilgrimage, by H. Snowdon-Ward (Black)
The Pilgrims' Road, by F. Elliston-Erwood (**Homeland Association**)
On the Pilgrims' Way, by D. P. Capper (**Methuen**)

NOTES

MAPS . .
MAPS . .
MAPS . .

YOU WILL NEED ORDNANCE SURVEY ONE INCH MAPS FOR YOUR WALKING TOUR

Every map mentioned in this book can be obtained from the Youth Hostels Association's London map department

---

GET YOUR MAPS FROM
Y.H.A., 22 GORDON SQ., W.C.1

www.ingramcontent.com/pod-product-compliance
Ingram Content Group UK Ltd.
Pitfield, Milton Keynes, MK11 3LW, UK
UKHW041417180426
11947UKWH00007B/187